ETHICS AND LEGAL RESPONSIBILITIES

Know Your Rights

A number of federal, state, and local laws are in place to protect employees' rights in the workplace. This table explains how these laws apply to break times, overtime pay, and salaried versus hourly employees. Many companies give breaks to their employees, even if the government does not require it.

Federal	The Fair Labor Standards Act (FLSA) regulates overtime pay and employee classification. This law guarantees employees at least time-and-a-half for their overtime work. (Time-and-a-half is when a company pays a worker 1.5 times their normal hourly rate.) The FLSA also classifies workers as nonexempt (hourly) or exempt (salaried). An employee's classification depends on details such as how much money he or she makes and the type of work he or she performs. No federal law exists to provide break time to workers. Employers must display a poster listing key terms of the FLSA in the workplace.
State	Eight states require employers to offer paid rest periods to employees. Some states provide additional overtime protections for employees. States may also create their own conditions for exempt and nonexempt status, providing more protection than those outlined under federal law.

Sharing your lunch break with co-workers can provide a great opportunity to get to know them better. It helps to build a sense of friendship. Friendly co-workers are more likely to support one another on the job.

Workplace Policies

GOALS

LEARN how company policies affect employees 8–11

INTERPRET company policies **10**

APPLY what you've learned to communicate effectively with your supervisor **11**

TERMS

policies

compensation

reimbursement

harassment

discrimination

Now that you have started your new job, you may have even more questions than you did before your first day. Questions like, "Who should I contact if I need to call in sick?" or "What should I do if I get hurt at work?" Luckily, your company has a policy manual to answer these questions. Following **policies**, or rules and regulations, can ensure success on the job.

A typical policy manual provides a lot of information to employees. It includes the company's position on many subjects and situations. By reading this document, employees can typically learn about the company's:

- structure or organization
- rules for employee conduct
- **compensation** (payment) procedures
- guidelines for use of company facilities or equipment

You should receive a copy of your company's policy manual from the human resources manager or your supervisor as soon as you begin your new job. The sample policy manual table of contents on page 9 explains how this information may be organized.

This section may include a company organization chart, as well as information about conditions of employment, conflicts of interest, performance reviews, and reasons for promotion or termination.

MIDWEST MANUFACTURING ENTERPRISES
Company Policy Manual

Here, you can learn about compensation (pay), pay periods, deductions, expense reports, and **reimbursement** (paying back) of employee expenses. It explains rules and options for employee benefits, such as health insurance and retirement plans.

The Attendance section describes working hours and schedules, how to clock in and out of work, break periods, calling in sick, and vacation time.

This section might explain the company's dress code, drug and alcohol policies, and rules about weapons and violence in the workplace. It may also detail rules about improper conduct.

This section explains rules for the use of company-owned computers, phones, and other property. It also describes safety procedures for operating company vehicles or machinery.

Employee Conduct

The employee conduct section of a policy manual is one of the most important. This section serves as a guide for how you should behave while at work. It outlines how the company expects you to dress, what behaviors are acceptable, and which behaviors are unacceptable.

Every workplace has policies that protect employees from harassment and discrimination. **Harassment** is behavior intended to disturb or upset another employee. **Discrimination** is unfair treatment of a person or group of people based on certain characteristics, such as race or religion.

You are responsible for following all policies, so read each page carefully.

Dress Code

Three of the most common workplace dress codes are a uniform, business or business casual, and casual dress. Even though it is restrictive, the uniform dress code is the easiest to follow. It lists exactly what you should wear. You may even receive your uniform from your employer.

Business or business casual dress codes can vary from workplace to workplace. Sometimes, men are expected to wear a suit or tie. Other times, women may wear dress pants and a nice blouse. It's best to observe what other employees are wearing and then model your dress accordingly.

With a casual dress code, you may be able to wear jeans and T-shirts. But you should never wear dirty or ripped clothing. You should also refrain from wearing T-shirts with comments or slogans.

ACTIVITY

▶ **Understanding Workplace Policies**

Study the examples from this company policy manual to the right. Then use the information to answer the questions below.

1. Could an employee that has a legal permit to carry a weapon bring that weapon to work at this company?

   _____

2. How would you summarize the company's definition of harassment?

   _____

   _____

3. Suppose a full-time employee began at this company on September 1. How many days of vacation pay would he or she have accumulated by the end of the year?

   _____

Company Policy Manual

- The possession, use, or sale of drugs and alcoholic beverages, as well as the possession or use of firearms or explosives, is strictly prohibited on company property.

- Harassment can be defined as conduct that shows hostility or aversion toward an individual because of his or her protected characteristic and that has the effect of unreasonably interfering with an individual's work performance by creating an intimidating, hostile, or offensive work environment.

- Full-time employees will begin accumulating vacation pay at a rate of one day per month, up to 10 days for the first three years of employment. Employees may carry over to the next year up to five days of unused vacation pay.

 To learn more about policy manuals, refer to the examples in *Document Literacy*.

Sometimes a dress code will be very specific. Other times you will need to use your best judgment to determine what to wear to work.

Uniform

Business Casual

Casual Dress

Working with your Supervisor

Your supervisor is your day-to-day contact for a variety of work-related information, including matters of company policy. He or she can advise you about policy issues. Your supervisor also may correct you if you violate certain policies, such as forgetting your uniform or failing to call in sick.

Of the many co-workers you'll come to know, none may be more important to you than your supervisor. Employees who enjoy strong relationships with their bosses can go far in a company. Those who don't, often don't. As a result, it's important to get to know your supervisor and his or her working style.

You can learn about your supervisor by observing his or her style of management. Look for both verbal and nonverbal clues in his or her interactions with employees. For example, does your supervisor usually act formal and professional? Does he or she seem friendly and approachable? Do people call this person by his or her first name, or by a title such as *Mr.*, *Mrs.*, or *Ms.*?

Next, use those observations to adapt your communication style to match that of your supervisor. For example, if your supervisor seems friendly and outgoing, it may be okay to say, "Hey Linda, I think we could use an extra cashier on Fridays." If your supervisor behaves more formally, you may wish to put your comments in writing.

ACTIVITY

▶ ## How to Communicate

Work with a classmate to model appropriate communication between an employee and a supervisor. For each scenario, take turns so that you each portray the employee and supervisor.

1. An employee must speak to his or her supervisor to call in sick for work. *(Hint: Give the name of the illness if you know, but don't share the details.)*

2. An employee must call his or her supervisor to explain that he or she will be late to work because of car trouble. *(Hint: Be honest. Everyone has been in this situation. If possible, say when you will arrive.)*

3. An employee must speak to his or her supervisor to request a day off. *(Hint: Depending on the company, you may not have to explain why you want a day off, although it may be granted if it's for a special occasion.)*

Procedures and Benefits

GOALS

INTERPRET company procedures 12

LEARN how company benefits affect employees . . . 14–15

WRITE an evaluation of two benefits packages and explain your choice of one over the other 15

TERMS

procedure

grievances

wages

deductibles

co-pay

In addition to policy manuals, many companies also publish procedure manuals. **Procedure** manuals give employees step-by-step instructions for completing important tasks. For instance, a construction worker might learn how to safely handle heavy machinery. A restaurant worker could learn how to comply with food safety rules. People with scientific or technical jobs may have a procedure manual for each task they perform. For example, a forensic chemist may have special procedures for processing different types of evidence. Examine the document below to learn more about policy manuals.

Hazardous Chemical Containers

Procedure manuals are typically divided into sections related to different aspects of a job.

Employees should label all vessels containing hazardous chemicals used in the workplace. These labels should include the name of the chemical, a hazard warning, and the name and address of the chemical's manufacturer.

Step-by-step instructions guide employees through important tasks. These instructions explain how an employee should safely handle hazardous chemicals in the workplace.

- If the label on such a container becomes unreadable or is removed, employees must find or create a replacement label for the container. Employees should contact their supervisor to receive blank labels to use as replacements.

- Employees working with hazardous chemicals transported through pipes should also contact their supervisor to obtain the following information:

    1. the names of the chemicals passing through the pipes

    2. the potential health risks of exposure to these chemicals

    3. the safety procedures required to avoid exposure to these chemicals, including the appropriate safety equipment to wear

Procedure manuals can also tell employees where to find additional information or who to contact for further assistance.

Learning Procedures

The size of a procedure manual can vary greatly, depending on the company. Some manuals might be only a few pages. Others could be more than 100 pages long. No matter the size, take your time when reviewing a procedure manual. Read carefully and make sure you understand it. If you are confused about a procedure, ask your supervisor to explain it further.

Procedure manuals cover many aspects of employment. These include safety procedures, such as wearing protective equipment and reporting accidents. Emergency procedures, such as weather emergencies and evacuation routes, also frequently appear in these manuals. Procedure manuals can also help employees handle tasks such as filing **grievances**—or complaints—and completing forms. An employee might wish to file a grievance regarding discrimination or a violation of workplace policies.

Employees wishing to take sick leave must also follow company procedure manuals. Suppose you have to call in sick to work. You may be assigned a contact person to notify that you are ill. When you return, you may be required to present a doctor's note excusing your absence.

Additionally, the Family and Medical Leave Act (FMLA) is a law that allows employees to receive unpaid time off for certain family and health-related issues. The act covers events such as pregnancy, child care, and adoption. It also covers employees who have serious health conditions or who must care for sick family members. Recently, the Department of Labor extended FMLA coverage to people, such as grandparents, who care for children even if they are not the mother or father. To apply for time off through the FMLA, employees must follow procedures outlined by their companies.

ACTIVITY

▶ **Procedure for FMLA**

Examine the steps listed below for requesting FMLA leave. Then number the steps in the correct order.

_____ 1. Employees should discuss the scheduling of their FMLA leave with supervisors, in order to possibly avoid the disruption of work.

_____ 2. If a supervisor determines any of the required documents to be incomplete or insufficient, employees must provide the missing information at least seven days before leave begins.

_____ 3. Employees should submit any necessary documents to return to work from FMLA leave in a timely manner.

_____ 4. Employees should submit requests for FMLA leave to their supervisors at least 30 days in advance (except in cases of emergency).

_____ 5. Before returning from FMLA leave, employees should contact their supervisors to develop a plan for their return to work.

_____ 6. Employees should provide all necessary documents for the certification and approval of requested FMLA leave to their supervisors at least 15 days before leave is scheduled to begin.

Both men and women can use the Family and Medical Leave Act to care for newborn or adopted children.

Employee Benefits

As an employee, you receive **wages** (payment or money) for the work that you do. Like many employees, you may also receive additional benefits from your employer. Some benefits are direct, such as healthcare and paid vacation. Other benefits are more informal or indirect. The table to the right explains some direct benefits.

Indirect benefits can vary based on your industry. For example, food service workers often receive free or reduced-price meals during breaks. Employees of cell phone companies may receive free phones and low-cost service plans. Retail sales associates often receive an employee discount that allows them to purchase clothing or other store goods at a reduced price. Some hospitality workers can stay in company-owned hotels or attend company-owned theme parks without paying full price.

Employers provide these and other indirect benefits so that employees are knowledgeable about the company's goods or services. Employees can then pass this knowledge on to customers. Have you ever asked your server to recommend a dish? Chances are he knows what he is talking about because the restaurant has allowed him to try food free of charge.

DIRECT BENEFITS

Benefit	Description
Paid vacation days	Employees receive a certain number of days that they can use for vacation, while still receiving their regular salary from their employer.
Healthcare benefits	These benefits often include health insurance for employees and their families. Companies may provide health insurance at no cost, or at a significantly reduced cost.
401(k) plans	These plans allow employees to have a portion of their wages directed to a retirement investment account. The wages that employees contribute to 401(k) accounts are not subject to income taxes.
Child care	Employers provide child care facilities for the children of employees during work hours.
Tuition reimbursement	Employers help pay for employees to take classes or receive additional training in areas related to their current jobs.
Profit sharing	An employer divides a portion of its profits among employees. Companies often base this payment on an employee's salary.

DL To learn more about workplace benefits, refer to the examples in *Document Literacy*.

Healthcare

More than half of all workers in the United States receive some type of employer-sponsored medical benefit plan. Employers offer many different varieties of coverage through these plans. When you begin a job, you should learn about the plans available to you. Your employer's human resources associates should help you become familiar with these options. They can also help you figure out the best choice for you.

When studying health benefit plans, you should always consider the types of coverage these plans provide. Some plans may only offer basic medical coverage. Others may cover vision and dental care, as well. Also, pay attention to the **deductibles**, or the amounts you must pay before insurance begins to cover your expenses.

Most employer-sponsored healthcare benefit packages cover prescription medications.

It's important to choose the best possible coverage for you, even if it's not the least expensive option. Co-pays may also influence your choice of health benefit plans. A **co-pay** is an out-of-pocket payment you must make each time you seek medical care. At times, you may need to change or update your health benefits or coverage.

Events like marriage, divorce, or childbirth can affect the type of benefits you need. Your employer should provide you with information about how to make any needed changes or switch plans altogether. If you change jobs or lose your job, you may also be able to buy extended health coverage through your former employer's plan.

ACTIVITY

▶ ### Health Plan A or B?

Work together with a small group to review the two health benefit plans shown here. Then decide which plan would work best for you. When you have made your choice, write a brief paragraph explaining which plan you chose and why you chose it.

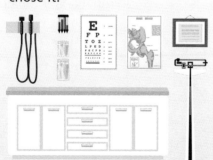

Health Plan A

- Employee Cost (monthly): $51.56 (Individual) / $344.30 (Family)
- Benefits: Medical, maternity, and chiropractic
- Co-pay: $15 for doctor visits and prescription drugs
- Employees can visit doctors of their choice
- Annual deductible: $0

Health Plan B

- Employee Cost (monthly): $45.36 (Individual) / $302.60 (Family)
- Benefits: Medical, maternity, and chiropractic
- Co-pay: $25 for doctor visits and prescription drugs
- Employees can only visit doctors in the plan's network
- Annual deductible: $500

Learning Your Job

TERMS

OSHA

mentor

lingo

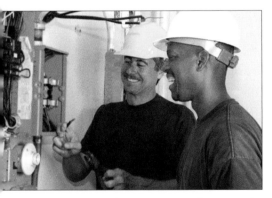

Apprentice electricians are often paired with a mentor for on-the-job training.

Marcus Davis arrived for his first day of work as a prep chef at Le Parisien. Marcus has a certification in culinary operations from his local community college, but this was his first time in a professional kitchen. Understandably, Marcus was nervous and had several questions. He wondered:

- Will I be asked to prepare foods a certain way?
- How will I know how to use the equipment in the kitchen?
- What if I'm asked to cook something I don't know how to make?

Fortunately, Marcus did not need to worry. Like many employers, Le Parisien ("The Parisian" in French) was prepared to train new employees without much experience. Employers train employees to teach them new or specific skills they will need to perform their jobs. Training might involve teaching an employee to use certain technology. For example, an employee may learn how to use a computer or a cash register. In Marcus's case, the restaurant manager might train him to use the restaurant's order-processing system.

Employees also receive training in how to operate equipment. This type of training may involve new and more experienced employees. When the equipment changes or new technologies are available, all employees will go through training. This is especially common for workers in medical and technological professions.

In skilled trade jobs, such as electrician and carpenter, new employees may begin as apprentices. Apprentices can progress to the level of journeyman or foreman as they gain experience.

COMMON TYPES OF TRAINING

Industry	Training Manual	Computerized or Video Training	Working with a Mentor	Apprenticeship or Probationary Training
Healthcare	✔	✔	✔	✔
Food service/retail	✔	✔	✔	
Technology	✔	✔		
Skilled trades	✔		✔	✔

Formal Training

Employers train employees in many different ways. Some provide written training materials. Others may assign an experienced employee to train new hires. Often, employees are trained using a mixture of formal and informal methods.

Formal training is more structured than informal training. Supervisors or heads of departments may conduct the training. It might be held in training centers, classrooms, or in the workplace. You may be required to pass a test to confirm that you've completed a portion of the training. You may be required to pass all components of formal training to continue in your job.

As a new employee, you should take an active role in your training. Determine which manual to use or the person you should ask if you have a question or problem. It's a good idea to take notes during any formal or informal training. You can refer to these notes later, as well as your other training materials. You should also figure out how to get more training when you need it.

ACTIVITY

▶ **Understand Training Manuals**

Read the excerpt from the training manual to the right. Next, write two questions about this training manual on the lines below. Then ask aloud two more questions to your classmate or instructor.

_____

_____

_____

_____

_____

_____

_____

SECURITY GUARD TRAINING MANUAL

Your responsibility as a security guard is to protect the company's employees and property. The most important duty of a security guard is to prevent problems from occurring. Security guards should remain visible at all times to discourage theft, vandalism, and injury. To succeed as a security guard you must:

REMAIN ALERT · *LISTEN* · *LOOK*

If an incident should occur, a security guard must follow these instructions:

1. Do not confront an offender.

2. Remain calm and observe what is happening. Write down your observations as soon as possible to help you remember what you witnessed.

3. Report the incident to law enforcement authorities, as well as to your supervisor.

Workplace Safety

In the course of your work, you will likely see safety warning signs like those in the activity below. These signs may warn you about a nearby hazard. They may also instruct you to take certain safety precautions. You should learn to recognize similar signs that you encounter through your work. By following the signs' warnings, you can help keep your workplace safe for you and your co-workers.

Safety warnings may appear in many different places throughout a workplace. The Occupational Safety and Health Administration **(OSHA)** requires that certain signs be posted as part of its safe workplace regulations.

You may be able to spot many safety warnings by the symbols or pictures used to illustrate their meanings. For instance, a picture of a person slipping and falling often symbolizes a wet floor. Including these symbols and pictures allows people who do not know the English language to understand the signs' meanings.

Safety warnings can also take the form of warning labels. A warning label might be attached to a container or to a piece of equipment itself. These labels instruct you on how to use equipment carefully and correctly. Labels often feature more information than warning signs.

ACTIVITY

▶ ## Safety Warnings

Study the signs and the information below. Then answer the question that follows.

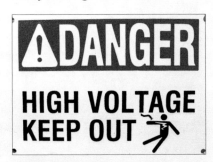

▶ Construction workers or cable television installers might see this sign. It warns about nearby electricity or electrical wires. Workers should avoid digging into the ground where dangerous power lines are buried.

▶ This sign tells employees that they should wear protective goggles in the area. About 2,000 work-related eye injuries occur daily in the United States. Signs like these encourage employees to prevent these injuries. Workers that might see these signs include scientists, technicians, landscapers, or metal workers.

▶ This sign alerts employees about a slippery surface where they might fall. Employees working on maintenance crews would likely encounter these signs frequently. Many workers in restaurants and bars, hospitals, and schools would also see these warning signs.

What types of warning signs might you see at your chosen workplace?

_____

_____

ETHICS AND LEGAL RESPONSIBILITIES

Protect Yourself

Wearing proper safety attire doesn't just keep you safe on the job. It's also a key part of working ethically. Employers are legally required to provide the safety gear employees need to do their jobs. If a company doesn't provide this equipment, it can be investigated and penalized. But as a worker, it is your responsibility to always wear the safety gear provided.

This becomes important when you consider the possible legal consequences. Suppose you failed to wear your safety attire one day and suffered an injury as a result. Because you didn't wear your safety equipment, your employer may not be held responsible for your injury. In addition to your injury, you could find yourself facing expensive medical bills.

Examine the photograph below. Pay close attention to the workers' location and the safety equipment they are wearing. What type of work do you think these people are doing?

Informal Training

You have learned about types of formal training that you might receive as a new employee. You can also learn about a new job through informal methods of training.

One common method is to work with a mentor. A **mentor** is a more experienced employee who offers guidance to a new employee. Mentors can help employees learn how to do their jobs better by providing informal feedback. They can also offer expertise that goes beyond what employees learn through their formal training.

At times, you may work with a mentor who behaves inappropriately. He or she might speak poorly of the company, your boss, or another co-worker. Should this happen, ignore this information and instead form your own opinions.

You will gain the most from this relationship by focusing on the positive advice a mentor can offer.

Many successful companies use mentoring as a way to develop effective employees.

Different Communication Styles

In your job, you may have co-workers who have different communication styles. One may be a "fast talker," while another may speak with a strong accent. Some may hover around you, but others may not check in with you at all.

It can be challenging when these communication styles differ from yours. You may have to ask a co-worker to repeat something she said quickly. Other times, you may have to ask a hovering co-worker to give you more space.

To succeed in your job, you need to be able to communicate effectively. If that means you need to ask a co-worker to check in with you more often, then do it. The key is to be polite and respectful. This will help aid communication and avoid conflict.

▶ PLAY VIDEO ❯

Mentoring This video shows how a mentor, Tina, provides informal training to a new co-worker, Jamal. When you have finished watching the video, answer the questions below:

DVD

Video 2

1. What information did Tina provide Jamal about his new job?

_____

2. How does Jamal take an active role in his training?

_____

3. What mistake does Tina make as a mentor? How should Jamal respond?

_____

4. How will Jamal benefit from Tina's guidance?

_____

Workplace Lingo

Every business or industry has its own set of lingo. An industry's **lingo** is the vocabulary that relates specifically to that particular field. When you start a new job, you may not know the lingo that goes along with it. However, your more experienced co-workers may use it frequently without explaining it.

As a new employee, you should always ask your co-workers to explain unfamiliar terms. You will also want to remember the words that you learn. That way, you can begin using them in your work.

Your mentor can be a great resource when it comes to learning lingo. You may not always feel comfortable asking other employees, especially high-level managers, to explain the lingo they are using. You may be embarrassed to let them know that you don't understand. But if you've established a positive relationship with your mentor, you will feel at ease asking him or her to explain the terminology.

COMMUNICATION

Learn the Lingo

Below are some examples of lingo from the healthcare, retail, and manufacturing industries.

Healthcare

a.c.: before meals (take medicine before meals)

appy: a person's appendix or a patient with appendicitis

bounceback: a patient who returns with the same complaints shortly after being released

CBC: stands for *complete blood count*; a blood test used to diagnose different illnesses and conditions

ICU: stands for *intensive care unit*

stat: immediately; right away

tox screen: testing the blood for drugs in a patient's system

Retail

brick and mortar: a retail store located in a building, rather than on a Web site or in a temporary location

comp sales: a measure used to compare sales revenue (income) in similar retail stores

cross sell: a sales approach in which a salesperson suggests an additional item based on a customer's purchases; for instance, recommending a scarf to go along with the purchase of a new coat

sales floor: the section of the store where merchandise is displayed and sold

SKU: stands for *stock keeping unit*; a number given to each item for sale that is used to track information about that item

Manufacturing

backlog: a build-up of tasks that have not been completed

batch: a set of items produced through a single process

plant: a factory or workshop at which products are manufactured

prototype: an original item from which additional copies are produced

quality control: a process that reviews the quality of all stages of production

r&d: stands for *research and development*; a process to develop new products or systems, or improve existing ones

Pathways

Technology in the Workplace

Workplace technology allows employees to work faster, better, and smarter. Today, almost every job features some type of technology. Retail workers may use a computerized point-of-sale (POS) system. Truck drivers may log their trips into a tracking computer or use a global positioning system (GPS) to make deliveries.

Sometimes though, such technology can confuse and even frighten new employees. However, it is important to understand how to use workplace technology. This knowledge likely will affect your job performance. For that reason, make sure that you receive training on all workplace technology. Ask for copies of instructional books or manuals, or to be retrained if you feel uncertain. You should embrace technology, not fear it. The following images and descriptions show how effective employees in many different fields use technology on the job.

▶ Law Enforcement

Law enforcement and other first responders must access information from a variety of locations. While possible, it would be difficult for them to carry procedure manuals, maps, and report forms out in the field. Instead, many law enforcement officers use laptop computers and handheld devices to assist them while on duty.

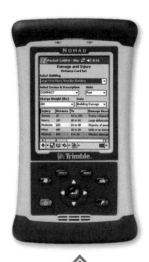

Handheld devices, such as this mini-computer, help officers locate information and file reports remotely.

INFORMATION TECHNOLOGY

Employees in the medical profession use technology to do everything from taking a patient's temperature to logging his or her insurance information.

▶ Medical Professionals

Medical professionals use technology to diagnose, monitor, and treat diseases or medical conditions. These technologies improve the quality of patient care. Medical technology aids in earlier diagnosis, less invasive treatment, and shorter hospital stays. Equipment such as ventilators help patients when they cannot breathe on their own, such as during an operation. Today's ventilator technology includes air capacity tube monitors and customizable computer screen interfaces. They allow medical professionals to monitor critical lung functions. Ventilators are also used in patient's homes, in nursing homes, or in rehabilitation facilities for patients who require breathing assistance.

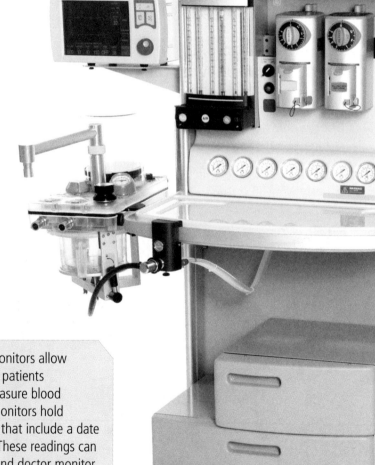

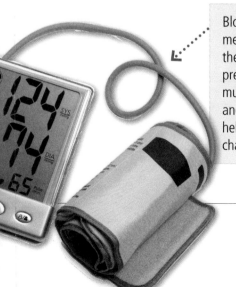

Blood pressure monitors allow medical staff and patients themselves to measure blood pressure. Some monitors hold multiple readings that include a date and time stamp. These readings can help the patient and doctor monitor changes in blood pressure.

▶ ## Transportation and Distribution Employees

Workers who move goods need to know where those goods are headed. Thirty years ago, drivers used printed maps. Today, they use a global positioning system, or GPS, device to get turn-by-turn directions to almost any location.

Plan a Route

Use a GPS device or an online mapping system such as Mapquest or Google Maps to plan the following routes:

1. a trip from your current location to your home

2. a trip from your home to a company with which you have applied for a job

▶ ## Agriculture, Food and Natural Resource Workers

What is the population density of your county? Is the land evenly divided between rural and urban areas? Data from a Geographic Information System, or GIS, can tell you! Workers in agricultural, food, and natural resource fields use GIS data and maps to measure information. Retailers, the banking industry, and government workers also regularly use GIS data.

Tractors operated by touch-screen consoles are becoming more widely used. These touch screens allow farmers to manage technologies that run their tractors, which include GPS guidance and satellite imagery.

ACTIVITY

▶ Analyze GIS Data

Natural resources are also measured and mapped using GIS data. Such information can help government departments and businesses. Analyze the map below of South Carolina's mineral resources. Then use the map to answer the following questions on a separate sheet of paper.

1. In general, where are most mineral deposits located?

2. Where might a cement company establish a factory near useful natural resources?

3. Based on information on the map, which business would be better off in South Carolina—a paper factory that uses commercial-grade Kaolin or a company that produces oil filtration systems that use Fuller's Earth? Why?

4. Based on information on the map, what conclusions can you draw about opportunities in South Carolina for businesses that use natural resources?

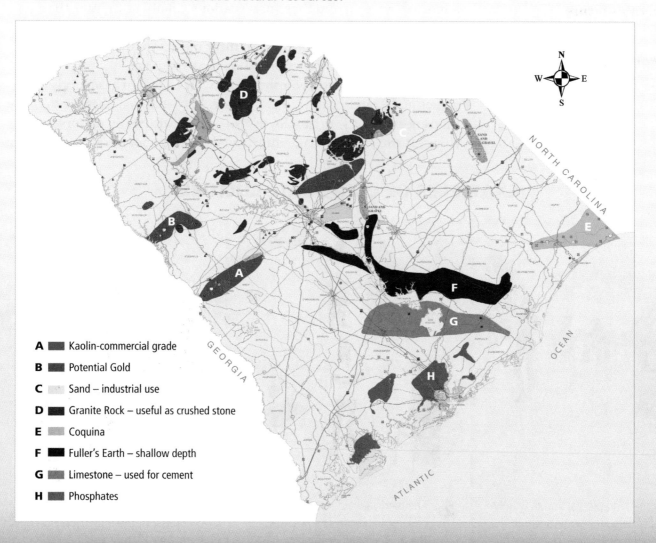

A ▩ Kaolin-commercial grade

B ▩ Potential Gold

C ▩ Sand – industrial use

D ▩ Granite Rock – useful as crushed stone

E ▩ Coquina

F ▩ Fuller's Earth – shallow depth

G ▩ Limestone – used for cement

H ▩ Phosphates

Corporate Culture

TERMS

corporate culture

infer

networking

One of the most important parts about how a business operates is not in any manual. Instead, the clues will be all around you. What is this mysterious set of guidelines? They are a company's corporate culture. A company's **corporate culture** is a group of often-unwritten values and practices that its workers follow. Some aspects of corporate culture might be stated, or hinted at, in a policy manual. However, many parts of corporate culture are unspoken. Over time, employees come to understand these practices and act on them.

Consider Shauna Taylor, who works as a cashier for a grocery store. On fall weekends, she notices that many of her co-workers wear football jerseys to work. She also notices that the store manager wears a football jersey. From these observations, Shauna can infer that, on fall weekends, it's part of the store's corporate culture to wear football jerseys instead of the uniform. To **infer** means to draw a reasonable conclusion based on the information that you have.

As a new employee, you should actively look for these kinds of values and practices in your workplace. Use what you observe to make inferences about your employer's corporate culture. By understanding this culture, you can make informed decisions about how to participate.

EXAMPLES OF CORPORATE CULTURE

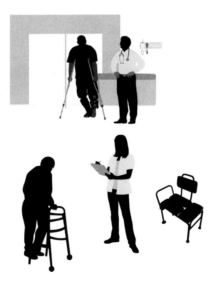

1 In some workplaces, you may only display personal items, such as photographs, in specific locations. At this workplace, employees may hang personal photos in the break room.

2 The medical field has a strict code of behavior. The physical therapists in this workplace call one another by their first names. But the doctor is always addressed as "Dr. Keller."

3 Department stores often award prizes for the employee who opens the most store credit accounts. Each store manager determines the prize, so these vary from store to store.

ACTIVITY

▶ Cultural Clues

Study the photos below. Then describe the clue about corporate culture that appears in each one.

A

_____

_____

_____

_____

_____

B

_____

_____

_____

_____

C

_____

_____

_____

_____

D

_____

_____

_____

E

_____

_____

_____

Corporate Culture Affects Employee Performance

Most companies use aspects of their corporate culture to affect employee performance. Companies may provide incentives for reaching goals. They may give small gifts to employees on a regular basis or reward the entire company with a large holiday party.

Meet Tim, a call center manager in Indiana. Tim's company values customer satisfaction, low call handling time, a high call volume, and strategies that increase their profits. The company often provides small gifts to their employees, such as stress balls, as recognition for doing a good job. One time they sent mirrors to each employee with the phrase, "Our customers know when you are smiling!" written on them.

One of Tim's goals as the manager is to promote positive behavior in the workplace. He wants to help his employees make and exceed their goals. He recognizes and rewards top employees. These employees become role models for the others.

Together with the other supervisors, Tim came up with the "I can help you with that" campaign. Whenever a supervisor heard a call center employee tell a customer "I can help you with that," the supervisor would give the employee a special card. This card allowed the employee to receive a free drink in the break room.

Whether it is a small gift like a free drink or the establishment of a company softball team, the most important goal of corporate culture is to have happy, productive employees.

ETHICS AND LEGAL RESPONSIBILITIES

Too Much of a Good Thing

Taking part in corporate culture can be both fun and rewarding. But you must also remember not to take it too far. This becomes especially true when socializing outside the workplace. In these cases, you might be tempted to participate in behaviors that you normally wouldn't do at work. Use your judgment and self-discipline to avoid drinking too much or having inappropriate contact with co-workers. If you have access to corporate perks, such as sports tickets or a credit card, use them responsibly. Remember, that your actions in these situations can have consequences—both in the workplace and in the legal system.

Networking and Socializing

Taking part in your company's corporate culture activities brings both opportunities and risks. It's important to understand these so that you can decide how best to participate. One positive way to participate is through networking. **Networking** is the process of building relationships with other people that will benefit your career. There are many ways to network. Participating in after-hours events designed to promote corporate culture is a good way to get to know people in the company.

Suppose that once a month a group of employees from a nursing home goes bowling. Douglas hates bowling, so he never goes. Sindi isn't good at bowling, but she recognizes that the point of the event is not to get the highest score, but to bond with her co-workers.

Often, Sindi shares a lane with the general manager, Nimah. Nimah sees how Sindi interacts with other employees and that she has a positive attitude. This is really the only face time that Sindi has with Nimah, and she's using it to her advantage. The next time Nimah has more shifts to offer or has a special project, she may think of asking Sindi.

Remember Shauna, who works at the grocery store that allows employees to wear football jerseys? If Shauna does not participate, some employees may feel that she does not want to be part of the team.

ACTIVITY

▶ Where Do You Fit In?

Socializing with co-workers is a great way to network. Certain aspects of corporate culture represent the fun, social side of working. But don't overstep the boundaries of appropriate workplace behavior. Remember that corporate culture includes the unwritten rules of a workplace. Because of this, management may not approve of some elements. Corporate culture can also unfairly exclude certain employees.

Answer the questions below as you consider how you might fit in with a workplace's corporate culture. Then discuss your answers with the group.

1. How would you learn about the corporate culture of your workplace?

2. What is one corporate culture activity in which you would feel comfortable participating? Explain your choice.

3. What is one corporate culture activity in which you would not feel comfortable participating? Explain your choice.

Chapter Recap

Using the list below, place a check mark next to the goals you achieved in Chapter 1.

▶ **In Lesson 1, you . . .**

❑ Learned how to overcome common concerns related to starting a new job

❑ Examined the effects of claiming dependents on a W-4 form

❑ Interpreted two different types of work schedules

▶ **In Lesson 2, you . . .**

❑ Learned how company policies affect employees

❑ Interpreted company policies

❑ Applied what you've learned to communicate effectively with your supervisor

▶ **In Lesson 3, you . . .**

❑ Interpreted company procedures

❑ Learned how company benefits affect employees

❑ Wrote an evaluation of two benefits packages and explained your choice of one over the other

▶ **In Lesson 4, you . . .**

❑ Prepared to do your job well

❑ Analyzed training manuals and safety warnings

❑ Learned how best to work with a mentor

▶ **In Lesson 5, you . . .**

❑ Learned how to identify aspects of corporate culture

❑ Analyzed images to determine clues to corporate culture

❑ Decided how you can comfortably participate in corporate culture

Chapter Review

Name: _____ Date: _____

▶ **Directions:** Choose the best answer.

1. What is the best way to find reliable information about an employer's rules and regulations?

   A. look them up online
   B. read the company's policy manual
   C. call the company's office for information
   D. ask a co-worker for information about specific rules

▶ **Directions:** Determine whether the following statements are true or false. If the statement is true, write T. If the statement is false, write F. Then rewrite the false statement to make it true.

2. With each dependent you claim on your W-4 form, the government withholds more money from your paycheck.

   _____

   _____

3. If a mentor criticizes an employer or co-worker, you should ignore this information and form your own conclusions.

   _____

   _____

▶ **Directions:** Write your answer to the question on the lines below.

4. How can an employee learn about their company's corporate culture?

   _____

   _____

▶ **Directions:** Match the terms in the left column to the correct definition in the right column.

_____ 5. dependent

_____ 6. lingo

_____ 7. mentor

_____ 8. networking

_____ 9. shift

A. building relationships with others to benefit your career

B. a more experienced employee who offers guidance to a new employee

C. a person who relies on another for support

D. a period of time during which an employee is scheduled to work

E. vocabulary that relates specifically to a particular field or subject

Chapter Review

Make a Fire Escape Plan

▶ **Directions:** Study this floor plan of a typical workplace. Locate the symbol that indicates the fire exit. Then use the prompts below to draw fire escape plans for different locations in this workplace.

10. Using a pen, mark the best fire escape route for a person in the warehouse.

11. Using a pencil, mark the best fire escape route for a person in the conference room.

Name: _____ Date: _____

Interpret Safety Warnings

▶ **Directions:** Look at the photographs of workplace safety warnings below and consider the meaning of each. Answer the questions beside each photo, and circle the piece of safety equipment that should be worn near these signs.

12. What does safety warning A mean?

   _____

   _____

13. If you worked in this location, what would you need to know in order to remain safe?

   _____

   _____

A

14. What does safety warning B mean?

   _____

   _____

15. If you worked in this location, what would you need to know in order to remain safe?

   _____

   _____

B

16. What does safety warning C mean?

   _____

   _____

17. If you worked in this location, what would you need to know in order to remain safe?

   _____

   _____

C

Chapter Review

Determine Wages, Deductions, and Take-Home Pay

▶ **Directions:** Suppose that the items below are your time card and pay stub.

18. Fill in the information missing from these documents (in the highlighted sections). Then use that information to calculate your take-home, or net, pay.

Name: _____

Week Ending: 6/13

Day	Morning		Afternoon		Total
	In	Out	In	Out	
Monday	8:55 AM	12:25 PM	12:55 PM	5:25 PM	
Tuesday	8:45 AM	12:15 PM			
Wednesday	8:45 AM	12:45 PM	1:40 PM	5:25 PM	
Thursday			12:35 PM	5:35 PM	
Friday	8:50 AM	12:05 PM	1:35 PM	5:50 PM	
Saturday	9:05 AM	1:35 PM			
				Total	

Name: _____

Week Ending: 6/13

Earnings	Deductions
_____ x $9.75 = _____ **Hrs Worked Rate Gross Wages**	Taxes.................$39.68 401(k).................$18.04 Health Insurance......$21.64 **Total Deductions** _____
_____ – _____ = _____ **Gross Wages Total Deductions Net Wages**	

Workplace Skills

▶ **LESSON 1:**

Being Professional
pages 36–39

▶ **LESSON 2:**

Working Effectively
pages 40–45

▶ **LESSON 3:**

Resolving Conflicts
pages 46–49

▶ **LESSON 4:**

Customer Service
pages 50–55

▶ **LESSON 5:**

Managing Stress
pages 56–59

Chapter Recap	Chapter Review
☑ _____	_____
☑ _____	_____
☑ _____	_____

▶ **CHAPTER 2:**

Recap/Review
pages 60–64

Being Professional

TERMS

professional

hygiene

self-discipline

direct reports

What does it mean to be *professional?*

Professional behavior means acting in a polite, respectful, and businesslike style while doing your job. This can include a wide range of skills and actions. For instance, you can outwardly show professionalism in many ways. Behaviors such as arriving on time for work, following company policies, and dressing appropriately show a commitment to being professional. Practicing good personal hygiene is another way to demonstrate professionalism. A person's **hygiene** is the way he or she stays clean and healthy. Brushing your teeth and showering are two important parts of personal hygiene.

Being professional also means taking direct responsibility for your duties at work and communicating effectively. Always focus on the tasks you are given. You shouldn't rely on your supervisor to keep you focused. Instead, you should check in regularly with him or her. This shows your professionalism, and it will help ensure success in your career. Communication with supervisors and co-workers is essential to being an effective employee.

ACTIVITY

▶ **Professional Behaviors**

This scene shows employees working in a retail store. Study the different parts of the scene by reading the labels. They describe what each employee is doing. Circle those employees who are behaving professionally. Draw an X over those employees who are acting unprofessionally.

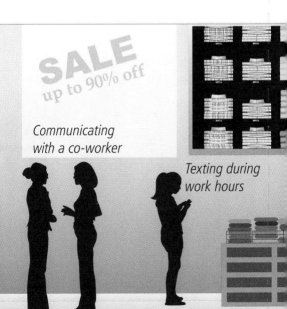

Socializing with a co-worker

Communicating with a co-worker

Texting during work hours

SALE up to 90% off

Professionalism Outside of the Workplace

It is important to remember that professional behavior is also required beyond the workplace. At times, you may be judged for your behavior even if you are not at work. Let's say you go to lunch with some of your co-workers. Even though you are away from the workplace, these co-workers may judge your behavior and table manners. If you eat fast or sloppily, make noise when chewing, or talk with your mouth full, they may think less of you. By acting professionally, you can avoid such missteps.

 To learn more about place settings and table manners, see Appendix D.

Sometimes, you need to act professionally even when you're not with co-workers. For example, imagine taking a trip to the mall with a boyfriend or girlfriend. Suppose that while you're shopping, the two of you get into an argument. If your supervisor saw you arguing, it might affect his or her impression of you. That is why it's best to behave professionally in public. You never know who you might see—or who might see you.

Like it or not, when you are in public, you may be evaluated by others. People form impressions about you and your work habits from the behaviors they observe. After all, you probably do it all the time, too! So be alert and behave appropriately.

LEADERSHIP AND TEAMWORK

Work Is *Every* Day

For an effective employee, professionalism and self-discipline often go hand-in-hand. **Self-discipline** means having the willpower to do the things expected of you. Keep in mind that when you take a job, you are making an everyday commitment to your employer. You may have days where you feel like staying home from work. For example, you might be tired or upset. In these situations, it is important to overcome these feelings, be professional, and go to work. Having the self-discipline to go to work—even when you don't feel like it—is key to keeping and succeeding in your job.

Folding clothes

Wearing clothes you would wear to a nightclub

Helping a customer at the cash register

Arriving late to work

SALE STARTS TODAY

Personal Professionalism

Professional behavior doesn't just refer to your job performance. Being professional also involves personal behaviors in the workplace. For instance, avoid taking part in workplace gossip. Keep personal opinions to yourself. This is especially true for topics that could easily offend a co-worker, such as politics or religion.

In general, you should avoid engaging in conversations that are unrelated to work. Such conversations take your focus away from your work. They can also lead to negative feelings and perhaps even trouble for those involved.

Professionalism often means removing personal feelings from the work that you do. You may have little in common with some of your co-workers. Others you may not like at all. Remember, though, that your co-workers are simply the people with whom you work in order to make money. You don't have to be best friends. But you do need to be professional and work together effectively. This is even true of supervisors, who must remain professional when working with their direct reports. A supervisor's **direct reports** are the employees that work directly for him or her.

Other employees in the workplace also should act professionally. As an employee and a co-worker, you should always be treated with respect. If you experience any harassment or discriminatory behavior, report the incident to your supervisor or to human resources.

▶ **PLAY** VIDEO ❯

Be On Guard This video shows two co-workers eating lunch together. As you watch, pay attention to their conversation.

DVD

Video 3

Then answer the questions below.

1. Which topics of conversation demonstrated unprofessional behavior?

   _____

2. What topic of conversation was an example of workplace gossip?

   _____

3. Would you like to work with these people? Why or why not?

   _____

   _____

At the same time, remember that everyone has a bad day once in a while. If a co-worker gets upset with you one day, give him or her the chance to apologize. You should never let someone else's behavior affect your attitude or your work. Remember to hold yourself to the same standards. Professionals take responsibility for their own actions.

TECHNOLOGY

Social Networking

In recent years, online social networking sites have exploded in popularity. If you're like many employees, you probably have a profile on one or more of these sites. Services like Facebook and Twitter can be great ways to keep in touch with friends and family. However, you should always think carefully about posting work-related information on these sites.

APPENDIX A — To learn more about using technology in the workplace, see Appendix E.

ACTIVITY

▶ Personal or Professional?

Read the descriptions and statements below. Then decide whether each exchange is personal or professional. Circle your response for each statement.

1. Dr. Roberts likes the way that Janie makes notations on his patients' charts. He asks her:

   "Janie, would you please show the other nurses how you've made these notations?"

   PERSONAL   **PROFESSIONAL**

2. Marina and Kirk get to work at the same time on Monday morning. Marina asks Kirk what he did over the weekend. Kirk responds:

   "I got so drunk on Saturday night!"

   PERSONAL   **PROFESSIONAL**

3. A group of employees is chatting while waiting for a meeting to start. An employee named Chris enters the room and asks the group:

   "Did you guys see the president's speech last night? I love this president!"

   PERSONAL   **PROFESSIONAL**

Employers continue to find new ways to monitor employees' use of these sites. Therefore, be sure that you don't post sensitive or private company information. Employers take these issues very seriously. You should also be careful about posting pictures of yourself going out with friends or to parties. Don't risk losing your job over a careless wall posting or tweet! This is especially true when posting from computers in the workplace.

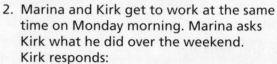

Similarly, you should avoid posting about work-related problems or disputes. Suppose you get frustrated with a co-worker or your supervisor. You might want to post a critical remark. But remember that these posts can often be seen by more people than you realize. Imagine what might happen if your boss discovered a negative work-related post on your Facebook wall.

Working Effectively

TERM

group dynamic

Think about the different groups you belong to in your life. Perhaps you thought of your family or your closest group of friends. Other groups might include a sports team you played on or a band with which you performed. Each of these groups has a group dynamic. A **group dynamic** is all of the different roles and interactions that make up a group. Every group will have both leaders and followers. This is true in most workplaces. Supervisors often act as leaders, while employees act as followers.

In these situations, it's okay to be a follower. The challenge in any group setting is to figure out how to make your personality mesh with those of the other members. The leader must make sure that group members work together effectively. It's also the leader's job to make sure that each person has a chance to contribute. Followers should speak up and contribute fully to group tasks. This is the best way for your supervisor to notice you and the quality of your work. Every employee needs to know how to work effectively within a group setting.

Workplace groups often include employees of different ethnicities and backgrounds. All must learn to work together.

ACTIVITY

▶ The Group Dynamic

For this activity, your instructor will divide your class into groups of four to six students each. Each group will then receive a jigsaw puzzle to complete. As you and your fellow group members piece together the puzzle, think about how you are working as a group. When your group has completed the puzzle, answer the questions below. These questions will help you analyze your group's dynamic. Then use your answers to discuss this activity as a class.

How Did You Do?

1. How did you work within your group? Did you act as a leader or as a follower?

_____

_____

_____

2. Did you work to help solve the puzzle to the best of your ability? Or did you sit back and allow others to do the work?

_____

_____

_____

3. Did you take control of the project and not allow others to participate?

_____

_____

_____

Your instructor will provide you with a puzzle.

4. How did you feel about working in a group? Did your group work together successfully?

_____

_____

_____

_____

Working Independently

Even when you work as a team in the workplace, you will often still have tasks to complete on your own. Think back to the puzzle activity on the last page. Did each member of your team take responsibility for a different section of the puzzle? Teamwork in many workplaces is like this, too. You might be responsible for a specific part of a larger project. In this way, you are working independently but also as part of a team.

Working alone has its advantages. It can give you a greater sense of independence and freedom. But it also carries greater responsibilities. Working alone requires more self-discipline than a shared project. You won't have other team members to encourage you and keep you focused on your tasks.

Use the following checklist to help you stay on track when working alone:

- ❐ **Make a schedule at the beginning of a task or project.** Decide how long you will need to complete each step and organize your time to account for this.

- ❐ **Create regular checklists throughout the project.** These checklists should be smaller, more specific versions of your overall schedule. These will help you stay on track and make sure you're not forgetting a step or falling behind.

- ❐ **Ask for feedback from your peers and supervisors.** Getting input from others will help you perform your job correctly. Your co-workers might also offer fresh ideas that could improve your work.

- ❐ **Keep your supervisor in the loop.** By updating your supervisor, you let him or her know that you are on track to finish the job. It will also provide him or her with an opportunity to share new or additional information about the project with you.

- ❐ **Allow extra time to check your work before you say it's completed.** Attention to detail shows that you take your job seriously.

Mark makes the pizzas by himself, but relies on Tommy to prepare the crust. Brooklyn, the cashier, needs Mark to make sure the orders are correct and on time.

Suppose you work as a stocker in a shoe store. You have been given the task of organizing the store's inventory. What if you don't understand certain parts of your assignment? What if you've organized some of the inventory but aren't sure you're on the right track? In a case like this, it's crucial that you ask for help and feedback. You should communicate with your supervisor to ensure that you understand your assignment. Talk to him or her before you begin and as you proceed. When you work alone, you have the sole responsibility for the outcome of your task. You'll be the one who receives any praise or criticism.

What if you are completing a part or step of a larger project on your own? It is very important to check in with other employees to make sure all of you are working toward the same goal. For example, imagine you are the nursing assistant responsible for bringing patients to examination rooms and taking their temperatures and blood pressures. You need to coordinate your schedule with the nurses and the doctor so patients don't wait too long. You may even have to find other tasks to do in between moving patients. Doing so will show that you are both a professional and a go-getter!

ACTIVITY

▶ ## Going It Alone

For this activity, follow the instructions below to make an origami swan. You will work independently on this task, and you'll have five minutes to complete your figure. When your project is complete, answer the questions below. These will help you to analyze how well you work on your own.

1. Begin with a square piece of paper. Fold the paper in half diagonally.

2. Fold the lower edges into the center crease of your paper. Then flip your paper over.

3. Next, fold the outside edges of your paper into the center crease.

4. Fold up the bottom point of your paper. Then, make a small fold to represent the swan's head.

5. Finally, fold the entire swan in half. When you pull the neck away from the body, the swan's body and head will unfold and reveal the finished swan.

How Did You Do?

1. How would you assess your performance on this task?

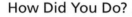

_____

2. Were you able to stay on task for the entire time period? Did you find yourself losing focus?

_____

3. Did you complete the task on time?

_____

4. Did you ask for help if you needed it?

_____

PROBLEM SOLVING/CRITICAL THINKING

Self-Discipline

The self-discipline you're expected to show in the workplace can be very similar to what you need when living on your own.

When you live alone, you are responsible for cleaning your own home and cooking your own meals. If you don't do it, no one will. You should approach your workplace tasks in the same way. Don't expect your co-workers to look out for you. Take ownership of the tasks you're assigned. Hold yourself accountable for doing your best work every day.

Pathways

Learning to Lead

Good leaders find ways to influence people by providing purpose, direction, and motivation. They do this to help achieve their company's goals. A supervisor's leadership style affects how a department or organization operates. This style also determines how issues are addressed and problems are solved. There are many types of leadership styles. The table below describes four of the most common styles. Read the examples and discuss the different leadership styles.

TYPES OF LEADERS

Leadership Style	Style Description	What This Leader May Say
By-the-book	In this style, all tasks must be completed according to procedure or policy. If the book doesn't cover it, the leader refers the issue to the next level above him or her. In this leadership style, the manager enforces policy rather than interpreting it.	"The company policy states that…" "I'm not sure if that is allowable but I will check and get back with you." "Work hours are from 8 to 5."
Hands-off	This type of leader allows employees great freedom in their daily duties. They must determine goals, make decisions, and resolve problems on their own.	"Whatever you think will work best. " "You two take care of the problem."
My-way-or-the-highway	In this style, leaders tell their employees what they want done and how they want it accomplished—without asking for input from their followers.	"Because I said so!" "Don't ask questions." "Just do it." "I didn't ask for your opinion."
Seeks Input	This style involves the leader including one or more employees in the decision-making process (determining what to do and how to do it). However, the leader maintains final authority on the decision.	"What do you think?" "I'd like feedback from everyone before I make a decision."

LEADERSHIP AND TEAMWORK

Strong leadership skills are important for any successful manager. But what makes a good leader, and how can you develop such skills? One strategy involves studying the behaviors of successful leaders. The following activities will allow you to examine, analyze, and understand both good and poor leadership characteristics. Remember these management roles in the future.

ACTIVITIES

▶ ### ACTIVITY 1: Take on the Role

Employee X works for a company that requires all employees to wear a uniform. However, Employee X is often improperly dressed at work. For example, some days Employee X wears jeans instead of the uniform's tan pants. On other days, Employee X is not wearing a nametag. Employee X's supervisor and co-workers are aware of the issue. Some co-workers believe Employee X's dress-code violations are the result of poor planning. Others believe the violations are intentional. If you were Employee X's boss, how would you handle the situation? To find out, conduct simulations using the following roles:

- Employee X
- a "by-the-book leader"
- a "hands-off leader"
- a "my-way-or-the-highway leader"
- a "leader who seeks input"

Place two chairs in the middle of the room. Facing each other, each leader takes a turn addressing Employee X's issues using his or her chosen leadership style.

▶ ### Group Discussion

1. Which leadership style worked the best?
2. What could each leader have done differently?
3. How would an "ideal" leader handle this situation?

▶ ### ACTIVITY 2: A Good Leader Is?

Think about leaders that you have currently or have had in the past. As a group, discuss and list below both good and poor characteristics of those leaders.

Good Leadership Characteristics	Poor Leadership Characteristics

Resolving Conflicts

TERMS

conflict

compromise

objective

chain of command

Workplaces can be busy, stressful places. They bring many people together, often in high-pressure situations. Given these facts, it is not surprising that many employees experience conflicts in the workplace. A **conflict** is a strong disagreement between people. Many factors can cause conflict in the workplace. These might include simple misunderstandings, poor communication, different working styles, or interoffice politics. Most people will experience a conflict with a co-worker. Conflict is a natural consequence of working with others.

Although workplace conflict is common, it should always be addressed. After all, simply ignoring conflicts will not make them go away. They are more likely to grow into larger problems. For this reason, you should learn to spot conflicts early. You can then take steps to resolve them quickly. Often, resolving a conflict requires people to compromise. A **compromise** is the settlement of a dispute in which each party gives up some of its demands. Both parties may give a little in a compromise since rarely is one person completely right and another completely wrong. The graphic below shows the steps to use in resolving workplace conflicts.

STEPS TO RESOLVE CONFLICT

1 **TRY** to determine the exact cause of the conflict.

2 **ASK** the employees involved to clearly express their sides of the dispute.

3 **ENCOURAGE** the parties to take a step back and consider the other person's view.

4 **INVITE** the employees to describe their ideal resolution of the conflict.

Consider how these ideals are alike and different. Brainstorm possible solutions that could lead to a compromise.

5 **CHOOSE** the solution that works best for everyone, especially the business.

ACTIVITY

▶ **Conflict Resolution**

Read the descriptions of workplace conflicts below. Evaluate each conflict from both sides. Then use the steps from the graphic on page 46 to suggest possible resolutions. Discuss your suggestions as a class.

SCENARIO 1: Samira and Tanya are medical billers who sit in cubicles next to each other. Samira is very friendly and outgoing. Tanya is quieter and keeps to herself. Samira makes business calls during the day, but she also makes many personal calls from her cubicle. This annoys Tanya, who finds the personal calls distracting. She begins to report Samira for policy violations, only some of which are true. Tanya is trying to get Samira fired.

_____

_____

SCENARIO 2: It seems that James shoots down every idea that Mickey has. James has been with the contracting company for more than 30 years. Mickey just received his electrical contracting license. James does not have a license, but has many years of practical experience. Mickey is beginning to feel that James will never respect him, so he does not treat James with respect. On the other hand, James is jealous that Mickey has a license. He is also upset because others at the company see Mickey as an authority on electronics, even though he's only been there a few months.

_____

_____

SCENARIO 3: Lloyd and Brittany, two X-ray technologists, are both hoping to be named head of the hospital's Radiology department. Because of this, both have been highly critical of each other's work. Both are excellent technologists and the problems they complain about are minor issues. Although the radiologists have no problems with the clarity of the MRI images, Lloyd and Brittany are constantly arguing. It's gotten so bad that other technologists have complained to the hospital's human resources manager about the conflict in the department. If Lloyd and Brittany continue in this way, neither will get the promotion.

_____

_____

Role of the Supervisor

Have you ever been in an argument in which both sides refused to budge? Perhaps the more you tried to work things out, the worse things became? When conflicts like this occur in the workplace, you may have to involve a supervisor to resolve them.

Often, employees will choose to resolve conflicts on their own. When you involve a supervisor, it makes the conflict more official. Your supervisor may be required to file a report. He or she may also have to discipline you or your co-worker.

If you decide that your supervisor should be involved in resolving a conflict, remember to express your point of view objectively. Being **objective** means dealing with facts without letting your feelings interfere with them. Also, focus on behaviors rather than personalities. Providing your supervisor with a list of a co-worker's offensive behaviors is more effective than insulting that co-worker.

At times, you may find that you actually have a conflict *with* your supervisor. In these cases, you will have to go further up your employer's chain of command to find assistance. A **chain of command** is the structure of authority within an organization. In some workplaces, you would contact a human resources official. In others, you might have to approach your supervisor's manager.

ACTIVITY

▶ Be the Supervisor

Partner with two classmates to act the scenario of a supervisor attempting to resolve a conflict between two co-workers. Use the character descriptions and details below to resolve the conflict.

- Employee A is a hard-working, experienced server at a popular local restaurant. He/she often pitches in to help newer employees as they learn about their jobs.

- Employee B is a new employee who has begun to take advantage of Employee A's helpfulness. Employee B does not work very hard, and counts on Employee A to pick up the slack. Employee A has finally had enough, demanding a share of Employee B's tips. Employee B argues that this is unfair.

- The restaurant manager must resolve the conflict between Employee A and Employee B. The manager should use information from the lesson to guide the workers to resolve their conflict.

Resolution: _____

_____

_____

LEADERSHIP AND TEAMWORK

Working With All Generations

Many seniors have decided to put off retirement. This means that four different generations—people born in the 1920s to those born in the 1990s—are together in the workplace for the first time.

Research suggests that a person's generation affects his or her attitudes, expectations, and motivations. This extends to the way that people think about—and perform at—work. As you can see below, these generations have a variety of nicknames.

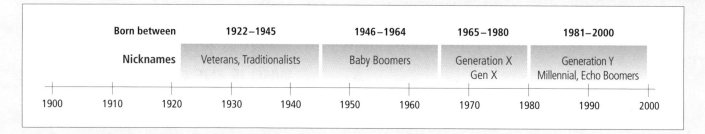

Born between	1922–1945	1946–1964	1965–1980	1981–2000
Nicknames	Veterans, Traditionalists	Baby Boomers	Generation X, Gen X	Generation Y, Millennial, Echo Boomers

1900   1910   1920   1930   1940   1950   1960   1970   1980   1990   2000

Different generations also behave differently in the workplace. These differences make it important that employees learn to communicate across generations.

You'll be able to resolve or even avoid conflicts if you understand how the generations differ. The table below explains the family dynamics and working styles of the different generations.

GENERATIONAL WORKING STYLES

	Veterans (1922–1945)	Baby Boomers (1946–1964)	Generation X (1965–1980)	Generation Y (1981–2000)
Core Values	Respect for authority; discipline	Optimistic; involved	Skeptical; fun-loving; informal	Realistic; confident; fun-loving; social
Family Dynamics	Traditional, two-parent household	Changing; some single-parent households	Dual-income households; latch-key kids	Multiple marriages; merged families
Communication Style	One-on-one; formal memorandum	Landline phones; in-person meetings	Cell phones; e-mail; person-to-person	Smart phones; mobile devices
Work Values	Hard working; duty before pleasure	Workaholics; personal fulfillment; question authority	Self-reliant; prefer structure and direction	Multi-tasking; goal-oriented
Leadership Style	Direct; firm	Treat people like colleagues	Everyone's equal; challenge others; ask why	(New to the workforce—no information yet.)
Means of Motivating	Respect their experience	Tell them they are valued and needed	Have them do it their own way	Tell them they will work with other bright, creative people

Customer Service

GOALS

LEARN strategies for providing good customer service . . .
. 50–53

EXAMINE ways to work with dissatisfied customers . . . 52–53

APPLY good customer service skills . . . . . .
. 53–55

TERMS

customer

active listening

paraphrase

support staff

What are some of the jobs that you picture when you think about customer service? You might first think of jobs in which an employee works behind a counter. These might include fast food or retail sales jobs. However, the definition of the word customer is actually very broad. A **customer** is any person or organization that buys or receives a good or service. Looking at it this way, a customer could be a patient in a doctor's office. A factory buying the parts you produce could also be a customer. As these examples show, almost every job involves some customer service skills.

Think about the fields in which you have worked. Who were your customers? How did you interact with customers in these fields? If you aren't sure who your customers were, look at the table to the right. It lists various types of jobs and some of the customers for each one.

WHO IS THE CUSTOMER?

Job	Customers
Farmer	Grocery stores, restaurants, families
Real estate agent	Home buyers and sellers
Drywaller	Construction companies, home owners
RN (registered nurse)	Patients in a doctor's office or hospital
Police officer	Citizens of a local area

COMMUNICATION

Professional Communication

The basics of good customer service apply to many jobs. Use the following strategies to offer good customer service in your field.

▶ Be Professional

Businesses depend on their customers to survive. You should always behave in a professional manner around customers. Remain calm and treat customers with respect. Behaving in a professional manner shows customers that you are serious about their business.

▶ Speak Clearly

Clear communication is an essential part of customer service. When customers have a problem, they want someone to help them quickly and directly. Customers can grow frustrated when workers speak softly or mumble. This makes it hard to communicate and solve the customer's problem.

TAKING CARE OF BUSINESS ASSOCIATES

The information technology (IT) department at this company is always busy.

Their customers are other employees at the company.

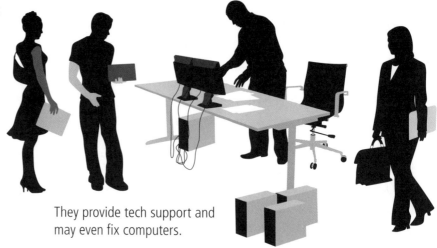

They provide tech support and may even fix computers.

Internal Customers

It's obvious that people standing at a checkout counter or waiting in a line are customers. But some people serve customers who are also co-workers. People who have these jobs are called support staff. **Support staff** include receptionists, secretaries, assistants, and information technology workers who support the work of other staff members. There are support staff positions in every field. Often, support staff work with both internal and external customers. For example, a doctor's assistant works for the doctor (internal) and the patient (external). It is important the he or she satisfies both types of customers.

Some people in support positions serve many internal customers. Let's look at Veronica, the administrative assistant to a company CEO. Her primary duties are to assist the CEO. But she works with other staff members, too. Veronica trains new employees on how to use computerized expense tracking and travel services. She also books travel for other executives. It's great that Veronica helps so many people, and she never neglects her primary duties with the CEO. It is important for any company to have strong support staff. Veronica is a great example of how people in those jobs can make a difference.

▶ Listen Actively

Active listening is listening carefully and responding thoughtfully to another person to show that you understand. You should always use active listening when interacting with customers. Active listening helps you think of a solution if there is a problem.

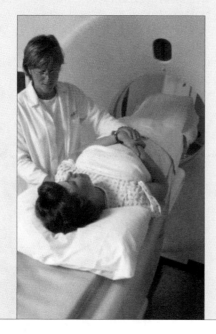

▶ Paraphrase

To **paraphrase** means to restate something in your own words. This skill proves useful in customer service because it can help you clarify a customer's feedback. By paraphrasing, you show that you understand their needs. This will help you solve problems more effectively.

Dissatisfied Customers

At times, both internal and external customers may become dissatisfied. This can happen when customers feel that they did not receive proper service. Others might be unhappy with a product they purchased. It is the customer service representative's job to make the situation right.

At some point anyone working with customers will have to work with a dissatisfied customer. The key is to listen to their issues and try to correct the problem. Always be polite and respectful, even if they are upset. If you handle the problem well, you may gain a customer for life!

J.T. is a customer service representative for a popular family-style restaurant called Marty's. One day, he receives a call from Hector Agosto. Hector's family had a negative experience the last time they visited Marty's. Read the transcript of their conversation to see how J.T. fixes the problem.

J.T.: Hello, thanks for calling Marty's. How can I help you?

HECTOR: My name's Hector Agosto, and my family and I were at your restaurant last night. It was the worst meal I've ever had.

J.T.: I'm so sorry, Mr. Agosto. Tell me what happened.
(By asking what happened, J.T. shows that he cares about Hector's dining experience. He also speaks respectfully to Hector.)

HECTOR: Well, the service was lousy. We waited 10 minutes before anyone even came to take our order. It was another 45 minutes until our food arrived. And when you have kids, it's really hard for them to sit still and wait that long. They shouldn't have to wait at a family restaurant.

J.T.: No, sir, they shouldn't.
(J.T. allows Hector to explain his frustrations. This shows Hector that J.T. is interested in what he has to say. By agreeing with Hector, J.T. is helping calm the upset customer.)

HECTOR: When the food did arrive, two of our orders were wrong. We just ate what we were served because we couldn't wait for the problem to be corrected.

J.T.: Mr. Agosto, I'm really sorry that you've had this experience. At Marty's, our goal is for each family to be served quickly and treated with respect. We expect every order to be correct. Please allow me to refund the cost of your meal. I would also like to give you a $25 gift card for your next meal at Marty's.
(By apologizing, J.T. seeks to lessen Hector's anger. J.T. also proposes a solution to make up for Hector's negative experience and encourage Hector and his family to eat at Marty's in the future.)

I'm also going to discuss this problem with our servers this evening. I'll find out why people had such a long wait. We will work to make sure it does not happen again.
(This is to convince Hector that if his family does return to the restaurant, the service will be better.)

HECTOR: Well, I appreciate that. I'll stop by tonight for the refund and to pick up the gift card.

J.T.: Thank you. I'll let the hostess know to expect you. Thank you, sir, for letting me know about your experience. If we don't know there is a problem, then we can't work to correct it.
(Thanking Hector for his call tells customers that their business and input are valued.)

← Hector, the customer

J.T., → the customer service representative

ACTIVITY

▶ ### The Unhappy Customer

Use what you've learned about working with unhappy customers to act this scenario with a classmate. One person plays the role of the customer, while the other is the server. The customer came to the restaurant at 2 PM Friday for a late lunch. He thinks he ordered from the lunch menu and should receive lunchtime prices. However, on Fridays the restaurant stops lunchtime prices at 2 PM. As a result, the customer was charged full dinner prices for his order. When the check comes, he points this out to the server and complains that he was overcharged. But he did receive the full dinner portion of food.

Remember the following to calm the customer and solve the problem:

- practice active listening
- ask questions
- apologize
- offer a solution

▶ **PLAY** VIDEO ❯

Customer Service Watch the video to see examples of customer service in action.
As you watch each scene, think about what you've learned about customer service.
Do the employees in the video demonstrate good or poor customer service skills?

Video 4

For each scene, circle **Good** or **Poor** to show your response. If you choose **Good**, write a brief description of what the employee did well. If you choose **Poor**, write a brief suggestion for how that employee could improve his or her customer service.

1. Good   Poor

_____

_____

_____

_____

_____

_____

2. Good   Poor

_____

_____

_____

_____

_____

_____

ACTIVITIES

▶ The Needy Patient

For this activity, you will also work with a partner. One of you will portray a busy Licensed Practical Nurse (LPN) working in a nursing home. The other will portray a needy patient at the nursing home. This patient spends a great deal of time talking to the LPN. This may prevent the LPN from completing his/her work duties.

Remember that you should be thoughtful when dealing with patients. It does not matter if you are at a doctor's office, lab, hospital, or nursing home. Patients are often worried, scared, upset, or in pain. This can make them difficult to deal with, so you must be kind and patient.

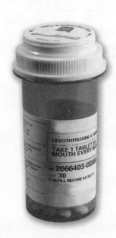

▶ Taking an Order

In this scenario, one person plays the role of an administrative assistant. The other acts as the owner of a landscaping business. The assistant is placing an order for landscaping work at his/her business. The landscaper needs to write down all of the necessary information and ask questions. For example, the assistant may ask for shrubs to be planted by the company's driveway. The landscaper may then ask what kind of shrubs the company would like and how many are needed. Each should paraphrase to ensure that they understand the other.

▶ Figuring the Total

Use basic math skills to solve the following word problems. Some of these problems ask you to calculate a percentage. A percentage is a part of a larger whole. It is expressed in hundredths. For example, suppose that 85 out of 100 cashiers use a calculator at work. We can instead say that 85% of cashiers use a calculator. You could also represent 85% using the number 0.85. Now suppose you wanted to determine 85 percent of the number 20. On a calculator, multiply 20 by 0.85— the answer is 17.

Percentages are often used in the workplace. You might be asked to calculate a percentage discount off the price of an item. You might also need to calculate a percentage tax from an item's price. Use your knowledge to answer the questions below.

1. Martha wants to purchase a T-shirt for $10. She can use her employee discount to take 20% off of the total price. How much will she pay for the T-shirt after using the discount?

_____

2. Nicolai runs the cash register for a local florist. He has to write up sales tickets and figure the amount of sales tax. His state charges 6.7% sales tax. If a ticket totals $32 before tax, what will the total be with tax?

_____

TECHNOLOGY

Making Math Easier

In your workplace, you may be responsible for tasks such as placing orders or figuring costs. These jobs require a lot of math. Computer programs have been developed to make these jobs easier.

You may already be familiar with Microsoft Excel®. Programs like this one can organize data quickly and efficiently. Excel can also rapidly perform complex calculations that would take people much longer to do.

Companies that use Excel can use AutoSum, functions, and fill-ins to create spreadsheets. These spreadsheets can track inventory, bills paid, and payments received. It is important to be familiar with calculators and computers. Almost all jobs today require some computer skills. If you take a basic Excel class, you'll increase your chance of landing a job or getting a promotion.

Even if you have taken an Excel class, it is important to stay sharp through practice. If you can't take a class, you should still try to practice working in Excel or some other spreadsheet or financial tracking system. Any computer that carries Microsoft Office® will feature Excel. You can find free practice tips and tutorials on the Internet or within the "Help" function of Excel itself.

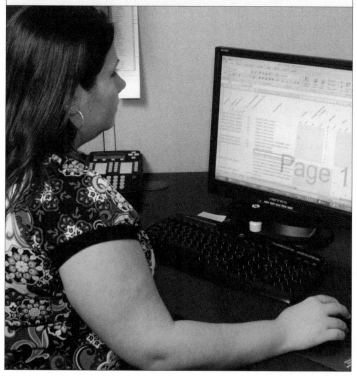

Managing Stress

TERMS

stress

stressors

Carmen Aprile's day was off to a rocky start. She had an argument with her daughter, who was refusing to get dressed for pre-school. When she finally dropped off the sulking girl, another parent noticed that Carmen had a flat tire. He was able to help her change the tire, but this made Carmen late to work. As she hurried inside, her upset boss asked, "Why didn't you call?" Carmen nearly cried at her station. What a horrible way to start the day!

Like many people, Carmen was reacting to stress. **Stress** is a condition that produces physical or mental tension. Events that cause stress are **stressors**. In this case, Carmen experienced several different stressors—all in the same morning. She became so stressed that she couldn't focus on her job. Pressures outside of the workplace caused Carmen to become stressed. Many aspects of a person's life can be a source of stress. People may feel stressed over financial or family issues. Even positive changes, such as getting married or having a baby, can cause stress.

It is important for effective employees to keep stressors outside of the workplace by focusing on their jobs. Carmen won't have to deal with her daughter's bad attitude or the flat tire while she's at work. The issues may still be there when she goes home. But bringing stress into the workplace will only make things worse.

ACTIVITY

▶ What Are Your Stressors?

Think about your daily life and routines. What causes you stress? As you think of stressors, consider how you react to them. For example, some people may become aggressive or angry. Others might cry or walk away. Stressors may cause others to shut down completely. By understanding how you respond to stress, you can better plan to manage it.

Evaluate your stressors and how you react to them. Using this information, work with your instructor to identify some safe ways to calm down when stressed. Organize these techniques into a written plan of action. Your action plan should list ways of coping with stress—both in daily life and on the job.

Handling Stress

Everyone feels stress at times. You can't always control when you might begin to feel stress. But you can control how this stress affects you. At times it may be tempting to just walk away from stress. But suppose you're an employee in a school, factory, or hospital. You can't simply walk away from your job responsibilities because of stress.

It's important to develop strategies to combat stress so that you can work through it and meet your responsibilities. The scenarios below show five examples of people dealing with stress in less desired ways. The text then describes a better way of relieving this stress. Which one of these stress relievers do you think will work the best for you?

Avoid physically acting out toward others. Instead, get rid of stressful energy by some other type of physical activity. Running or lifting weights both can help to relieve stress.

At times, stress may cause you to exaggerate, or overstate, a problem. Rather than continue to make the problem bigger, take a step back. If possible, try to sleep on the problem. With a bit of time and distance, the problem may seem more manageable.

Don't become either emotionally withdrawn or overly emotional. Instead, try to relax and focus on the specifics of the problem. This might include praying or meditating. You might also go for a hike, take a long bath, or listen to music.

Refrain from abusing cigarettes or alcohol to cope with stress. Instead, try speaking to a friend, family member, mentor, or spiritual advisor about the causes of your stress.

Sometimes you may be tempted to take your stress out on others. Instead of creating conflict with others, try to be honest with them about your feelings. Instead of arguing with them, try discussing the real issues that are causing you stress. Friends and family members will be supportive if you are honest with them about the root of the problem.

Stress on the Job

You may find your job to also be a source of stress. Feeling overworked or undertrained can produce stress. Conflict with a supervisor or co-worker can also act as a stressor. As in daily life, you should look for ways to ease the stress you feel in the workplace. Seek out the best way to let others know that you are feeling stressed. You might alert your supervisor, or perhaps a human resources manager. By acknowledging that you feel stressed, your fellow employees can begin to help you find relief.

▶ PLAY VIDEO ❯

What Would You Do?

The following video shows an employee facing a stressful situation in the workplace. As you watch the video, try to identify her stressors and positive ways for her to deal with the stress.

DVD

Video 5

Your instructor will pause the video after Part I to give you a chance to discuss the situation.

Answer these questions after watching Part I.

1. What causes Quanda to become stressed?

_____

2. How do you know that Quanda is stressed?

_____

3. What would be a more positive way for her to react?

_____

Answer these questions after watching Part II.

4. How does Quanda handle the situation this time?

_____

_____

5. How might you react if you were in Quanda's situation?

_____

_____

PROBLEM SOLVING/CRITICAL THINKING

Finding Workable Solutions

Study the images and read the captions to learn about potential ways to handle stress in the workplace.

▶ Airline Worker

This airline worker faces a long line of impatient customers. To alleviate her stress, she should alert her co-workers and supervisor to this situation. She should ask them for help so that the customers' needs can be met quickly.

This flight attendant finds that her fellow crewmembers often leave her behind in the terminal. They walk ahead as a group and she cannot catch them. The crewmembers tell the flight attendant when they are planning to leave the break room, but she is seldom ready when they are. She should realize that her behavior is the problem and try to be on time in the future.

▶ Cook/Chef

These cooks have been asked by the restaurant manager to work late. It has been a busy evening and they are angry about staying late. Rather than lashing out, they instead should take a break to calm down and refocus. Then they can return to their stations and finish the night's work without additional stress.

The restaurant's servers have not given this chef the information he needs to prepare orders correctly. Rather than snapping at the servers, the chef should explain the problem calmly and clearly. He needs to tell the wait staff how this problem affects him. Then he can better convince them to change their behavior.

▶ Carpenter

This carpenter is stressed because she has not been properly trained to operate a workplace machine. To ease her stress, she should contact her supervisor to request the proper training. Taking safety risks by operating unfamiliar equipment will only cause more stress and may be dangerous.

This carpenter and a co-worker disagree about how to perform a task. To relieve this stress, the carpenter should seek out a foreman. She can help the carpenters resolve the dispute quickly and prevent an already stressful situation from getting worse.

CHAPTER 2

Chapter Recap

Using the list below, place a checkmark next to the goals you achieved in Chapter 2.

▶ In Lesson 1, you . . .

- ❐ Learned how to demonstrate professional behavior
- ❐ Decided which behaviors are appropriate and inappropriate in the workplace
- ❐ Examined the difference between personal and professional communications

▶ In Lesson 2, you . . .

- ❐ Learned about group dynamics
- ❐ Examined your performance in group and individual activities
- ❐ Studied strategies for working effectively as an individual

▶ In Lesson 3, you . . .

- ❐ Learned the steps to resolve workplace conflict
- ❐ Analyzed situations to determine the root of the conflict and the best solution
- ❐ Applied information about the role of the supervisor in resolving conflicts

▶ In Lesson 4, you . . .

- ❐ Learned strategies for providing good customer service
- ❐ Examined ways to work with dissatisfied customers
- ❐ Applied good customer service skills

▶ In Lesson 5, you . . .

- ❐ Learned about stress and its causes
- ❐ Completed a plan for combating stress in your daily life and on the job
- ❐ Examined stress in the workplace and strategies to relieve it

CHAPTER 2

Chapter Review

Name: _____ Date: _____

▶ **Directions:** Choose the best answer.

1. Which of the following is an appropriate way of relieving workplace stress?

   A. abusing cigarettes or alcohol
   B. taking a deep breath and finding help
   C. walking away from your workplace
   D. physically acting out toward your co-workers

▶ **Directions:** Determine whether the following statements are true or false. If the statement is true, write T. If the statement is false, write F. Then rewrite the false statement to make it true.

2. Working in a group requires more self-discipline than working independently.

   _____

   _____

3. Almost every job requires employees to use some type of customer service skills.

   _____

   _____

▶ **Directions:** Write your answer to the question on the lines below.

4. Why is it important to show professionalism outside of the workplace?

   _____

   _____

   _____

▶ **Directions:** Match the terms in the left column to the correct definition in the right column.

_____ 5. chain of command

_____ 6. compromise

_____ 7. group dynamic

_____ 8. hygiene

_____ 9. professional

A. to give up something that you want in exchange for something else

B. polite, respectful, and businesslike behavior

C. the structure of authority in an organization

D. the ways that a person stays clean and healthy

E. the roles and interactions of people working together

Chapter Review

Using a Filing System

▶ **Directions:** As you may have noticed on your last visit to the doctor, medical charts are often coded using both letters and numbers. Use the following information to help the medical assistants in Dr. Kaauwai's office file their patients' charts.

In this office, patients are coded based on the first two letters of their last name, and the first letter of their first name. This patient's name is **S**helby **Wr**ight.

W
R
S

Each patient is also assigned a number. The first patient at this office was number 1000, the next one 1001, and so on.

2
3
5
7

10. Dr. Kaauwai has a new patient named Jadene Luta. The last new patient's number was 3691. How should Jadene's file be labeled?

11. Where should Joey Lui's chart be filed?

A. Between LUA1037 and LUJ1118

B. Between LUH2739 and LUL3054

L
U
J
1
2
6
4

12. Where should Farah Gaston's chart be filed?

A. Between FIL3624 and GLP2498

B. Between FAF2308 and FAS2403

G
A
F
2
3
6
7

13. Where should Ayannah Coffey's chart be filed?

A. Between COA1513 and COA3177

B. Between COA2990 and COA3518

C
O
A
2
9
8
5

Name: _____ Date: _____

Processing Returns

▶ **Directions:** Suppose you work as a cashier in a clothing store. You could provide good customer service in a number of ways. One way is by handling customer returns. Look at the receipts below. Each contains the store's return policy, as well as details about the individual customers' purchases. Use the information on the receipts to answer the questions.

For Receipt A, the customer comes to the store on July 12, 2011, and wants to return the baseball cap that he purchased.

14. Based on the store's return policy, what can you do for this customer?

_____

_____

15. How should you present this information to the customer and overcome any of his objections?

_____

_____

For Receipt B, the customer comes to the store on Oct ober 14, 2011, and wants to return the jeans that she purchased.

16. Based on the store's return policy, what can you do for this customer?

_____

_____

17. How should you present this information to the customer and overcome any of her objections?

_____

Receipt A

DESIGNER OUTFITTERS
5425 Wilshire Blvd.
Los Angeles, CA
(555) 555-1111

Sale # 347		07/10/11
QTY	SKU	PRICE
1	baseball cap 060875	$17.99
	Tax 9.75%	$1.75
	TOTAL	$19.74
Payment: CHECK		$19.74

Check # 224

RETURN POLICY

RETURNS WILL ONLY BE ACCEPTED WITHIN 30 DAYS OF PURCHASE

CREDIT CARD: Customer will receive a refund to their credit card account.

DEBIT CARD: Customer will receive a cash refund.

PERSONAL CHECK: Customer will receive a store credit if returning item less than 7 business days after purchase. Customer will receive a cash refund if returning item more than 7 business days after purchase.

Receipt B

DESIGNER OUTFITTERS
5425 Wilshire Blvd.
Los Angeles, CA
(555) 555-1111

Sale # 598		09/22/11
QTY	SKU	PRICE
1	jeans 042580	$29.99
2	earrings	$9.99 ea
	Tax 9.75%	$4.87
	TOTAL	$54.84
Payment: CREDIT		$54.84

Card No. xxxx5655

RETURN POLICY

RETURNS WILL ONLY BE ACCEPTED WITHIN 30 DAYS OF PURCHASE

CREDIT CARD: Customer will receive a refund to their credit card account.

DEBIT CARD: Customer will receive a cash refund.

PERSONAL CHECK: Customer will receive a store credit if returning item less than 7 business days after purchase. Customer will receive a cash refund if returning item more than 7 business days after purchase.

Customers often are tense when returning items. However, employees must follow their store's return policy. Your challenge is to present the policy in a positive way and satisfy the customer.

Taking and Leaving Messages

▶ **Directions:** A key part of your job may involve taking messages.

18. In this activity, work with a classmate to practice leaving and writing phone messages. You and your partner will take turns using the phone scripts on this page to leave a message. While your partner gives his or her message, write it down on the memo pad. Take turns until you both have written all of the details of your partner's message.

**" ... **

MESSAGE A: I would like to hire a disc jockey for a wedding reception.

The wedding will take place on Saturday, September 25. The reception will begin at 7:00 PM.

I need to know if you are available to DJ that evening.

I need to know your rates and fees.

I need to leave an email address where I can be reached at any time.

" ...

" ...

MESSAGE B: I am searching for a new landscaping service to care for my lawn.

I need to know how much it will cost for weekly mowing and trimming of my yard.

I want to know how soon your service could start tending to my lawn.

I want to know if you offer any additional services, such as weed control.

I need to leave a home and work phone number.

Home: (734) 555-3461

Work: (734) 555-8883

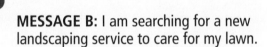

FOR _____			Urgent ☐

DATE _____ TIME _____ A.M. / P.M.

While You Were Out

M _____

OF _____

PHONE _____
AREA CODE　　　NUMBER　　　EXTENSION

TELEPHONED		PLEASE CALL	
CAME TO SEE YOU		WILL CALL AGAIN	
RETURNED YOUR CALL		WANTS TO SEE YOU	

MESSAGE _____
_____
_____
_____
_____
_____
_____

SIGNED _____

adams 9711

CHAPTER 3

Job Performance

▶ **LESSON 1:**

Self-Esteem on the Job

▶ **LESSON 2:**

Feedback

▶ **LESSON 3:**

Performance Assessment

Chapter Recap	Chapter Review
☑ _____	_____
☑ _____	_____
☑ _____	_____

▶ **CHAPTER 3:**

Recap/Review

Self-Esteem on the Job

TERM

self-esteem

Jennifer Matsuda couldn't stop smiling as she rode the bus home from work. Jennifer works as a veterinary technician. Earlier that day, a family brought their dog into the vet's office. Jennifer was the first employee in the office to see the dog. She quickly realized that he was very sick and alerted the veterinarian. The veterinarian then rushed the dog into emergency surgery and saved his life.

After the operation, the veterinarian praised Jennifer. "My boss said that if I hadn't made quick, smart decisions, the dog probably wouldn't have made it," she recalled. This achievement boosted Jennifer's self-esteem. **Self-esteem** is a feeling of confidence and satisfaction with oneself.

Like Jennifer, many people build self-esteem through their accomplishments. These might occur in the workplace or in daily life. Having positive self-esteem can prove useful in any setting. This confidence gives you the energy and enthusiasm to succeed!

ACTIVITY

▶ Your Own Personal Cheerleader

An important part of building self-esteem comes in recognizing and taking pride in your own accomplishments. Think back over your lifetime. What are some of your proudest moments? Perhaps it was graduating from high school or teaching your child to read. Try to recall both personal and professional accomplishments. Then list or draw these accomplishments on a separate sheet of paper.

You Are Valued

You may know workers who complain about their employers. They may distrust the companies for which they work. Perhaps they've told you that their companies view employees only as numbers.

In reality, most companies truly value their employees. Successful businesses invest both time and money developing effective employees. As a result, companies want their workers to succeed. You shouldn't think that your employer doesn't support you. Employers work hard to keep good employees, not drive them away.

Meet Amy, the manager of a local community bank. Amy values her employees because *their* work helps *her* bank succeed. "Whenever I get a compliment from the home office, I say, 'if you value me, you value my employees.' We are all in it together. We are all parts of the whole."

Amy acknowledges that while a few managers may be out for themselves, most of them are positive people. She tells her employees, "I don't want to bring you down; I want to applaud you. I want to recognize what you do well and work with you to improve the areas that are scary for you or difficult for you. I see when you struggle; be open and accept my feedback and you can go far!"

Whether through giving awards or simply by showing their gratitude, you should understand that employers appreciate the work you do every day.

Several of Amy's employees have been promoted to jobs at the home office. Instead of being upset at losing them, Amy and the rest of her staff feel proud and wish them well. To Amy, that is the ultimate success. She herself began as a teller and is now a vice-president. One day her bank manager offered her the chance to attend marketing classes. He chose Amy because her positive attitude was helping to market the bank every day!

As a manager, Amy says, "It's very comforting to see the lights come on and to recognize the potential in people. I don't want to start over with a new employee. I want to work with the person who is putting in the effort."

Work Increases Self-Esteem

Reyna is a phlebotomist (a medical worker who draws blood samples from patients). Several of her job skills add to her sense of self-esteem, both personally and at work.

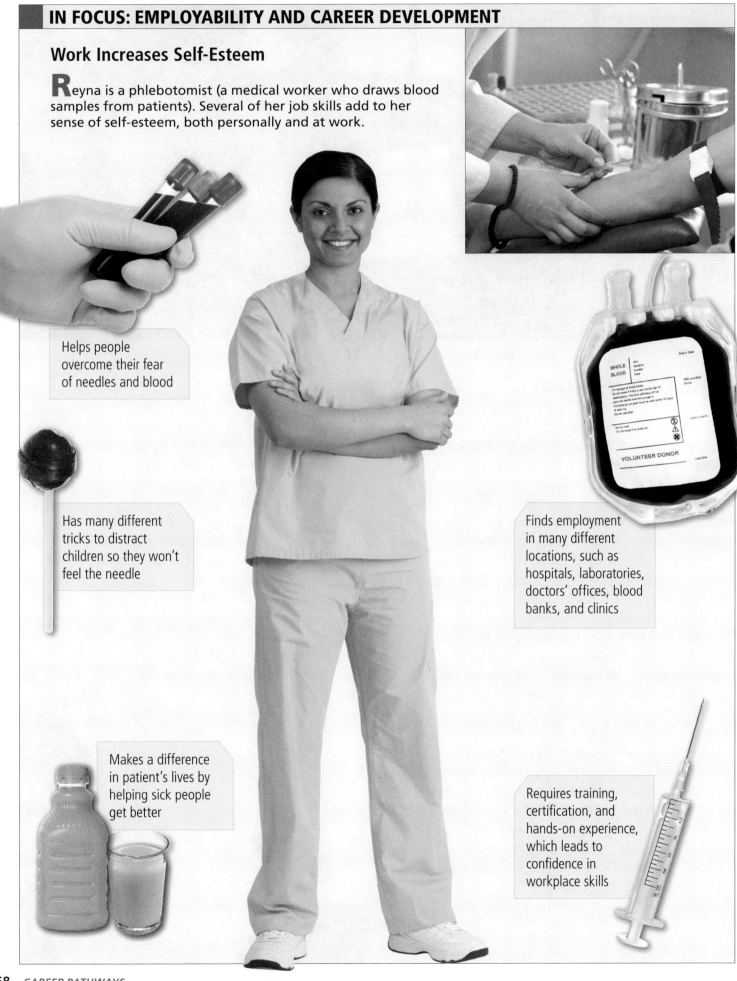

Helps people overcome their fear of needles and blood

Has many different tricks to distract children so they won't feel the needle

Makes a difference in patient's lives by helping sick people get better

Finds employment in many different locations, such as hospitals, laboratories, doctors' offices, blood banks, and clinics

Requires training, certification, and hands-on experience, which leads to confidence in workplace skills

Self-Esteem on the Job

Many employees struggle with self-esteem in the workplace. This is especially true of new employees. Fortunately, there are ways to build your self-esteem in the workplace. These strategies can help you to gain confidence and stay positive in your job.

For instance, you can build self-esteem simply by behaving confidently. When you believe in yourself, your co-workers will take notice. You can behave confidently by speaking strongly and clearly. You can also carry yourself with a confident posture. These may seem like small steps to take. But over time, the positive feelings they generate will help improve your self-esteem.

Another effective way of building self-esteem involves your interactions with co-workers. Have you ever noticed that positivity can be contagious in the workplace? Positive people tend to stick together. They also tend to avoid negative people.

Try to associate with positive people. They are more likely to offer encouragement and support that will help build your self-esteem. At the same time, you should offer encouragement and support to others.

Don't discount small achievements. You can build self-esteem by setting daily workplace goals. For instance, a server might decide, "Today, I'm going to convince five of my customers to order dessert." A hospital orderly might think, "Today, I'm going to remember something special about each of my regular patients." Make a checklist of the goals you set for yourself. Then check off each goal as you achieve it. Remember that no goal is too small to build self-esteem.

You should feel proud every time you accomplish something at your job. Whether it's answering the phone politely or handling a difficult customer, every accomplishment will help to boost your self-esteem.

PROBLEM SOLVING/CRITICAL THINKING

Keep Your Focus

In Chapter 2, you learned that outside stressors can have a harmful effect on your performance at work. The same holds true for self-esteem.

When personal problems threaten to lower your self-esteem, try to separate these struggles from your work performance. For instance, you might be upset over a breakup with a girlfriend or boyfriend. Perhaps you've had an argument with a friend and feel upset about things that were said during it. You may feel depressed and wish to sulk through your workday. However, it's important that you don't allow these feelings to influence your work.

Remember that your employer's focus remains on your job performance, not on your personal situations. Even though it may be difficult, try not to let personal issues that may lower your self-esteem affect your job. If you continue to perform your job well, your workplace self-esteem should remain high. Feeling good about your work might even help you work through difficult times in your personal life.

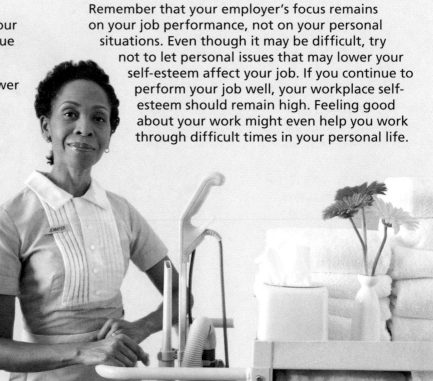

Feedback

TERMS

constructive feedback

sensitive

Feedback is a word that can strike fear in the hearts of many employees. You may learn that you'll be receiving feedback and picture your supervisor criticizing you. But feedback isn't meant to put you down. Instead, it shows you ways in which you can grow as an employee. In fact, effective employees welcome constructive feedback. Employers provide **constructive feedback** to address workplace performance issues and encourage improvement and growth.

Meet Rae, who works at a lab that builds dentures. Rae's supervisor monitors her work and sometimes corrects what she is doing. Rae understands that he is making sure the product is built correctly, rather than picking on her.

While you need to accept negative feedback, you should also focus on positive feedback from your supervisor about what you are doing right. Take pride in what you've done well. You should also work to correct the issues noted by your supervisor. Remember that supervisors only give you constructive feedback to help you improve. In this lesson, you will learn strategies for receiving and using feedback, and how to give feedback to others.

Sometimes feedback is given informally, such as while you are working. Other times, your supervisor may meet with you privately to provide more formal feedback. You should always have the chance to respond to feedback. In doing so, you should remain calm and professional.

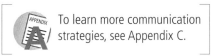 To learn more communication strategies, see Appendix C.

Handling Feedback

Because feedback is a part of every job, it's important that you learn how to handle it properly. By following some basic guidelines, you can make sure that you won't let feedback negatively affect your work.

The most important strategy for handling feedback effectively is to remain objective. Don't get defensive about the suggestions your supervisor makes. You will gain more from feedback if you keep an open mind. Be honest with yourself and you'll find that your supervisor often makes a good point.

You should also remember not to take feedback personally. Constructive feedback can be difficult to hear. At times, it may seem like your supervisor is insulting you. Remember, though, that feedback reflects your work-based behaviors, not your personal qualities.

Finally, don't let your nerves get in the way of receiving and understanding feedback. Receiving feedback can be a stressful process, and it's natural to feel nervous. Try instead to take a deep breath and focus on the points that your supervisor is trying to make. Don't be afraid to ask him or her to repeat or explain details about your workplace performance. It's important for you to understand the feedback so that you can put it into action.

It's okay to be sensitive when you receive feedback. When you are **sensitive**, it means that the attitudes and feelings of others affect you. This shows that you care about your work. It is most important, though, that you learn to accept feedback and use it to improve your job performance. Remember, if your supervisor didn't care about your performance, he or she wouldn't bother to give you feedback. Providing feedback shows that your employer values your work and wants to invest in making you a more effective employee. Below are examples of the types of informal feedback you might receive in the workplace:

- informal one-on-one meetings with a supervisor
- team meetings or conferences
- notes (handwritten or typed)
- computer-generated reports on employee productivity
- e-mail remarks about a task or product

Who knows? By having an open mind, you may even be grateful for the feedback your supervisor provides.

COMMUNICATION

Listening Through Stress

Stressful situations can make it hard to listen carefully. If you are worried or upset about receiving feedback, it may be difficult for you to concentrate. Because of this, you may want to use listening strategies to help you process, remember, and apply the feedback you receive.

For example, start by maintaining eye contact with your supervisor. This will help you stay focused on what he or she is saying. Also, try repeating your supervisor's words in your head. This will help reinforce what you are hearing. It will also help you determine whether you need to ask your supervisor to repeat something you didn't understand.

You may find it helpful to take notes during your conversation. These notes will help you remember the information you hear. It will also give you a written record of the feedback you receive. Writing feedback down can also make it seem less personal.

Formal Feedback You have already learned some of the ways to receive informal feedback. Your supervisor will also give you formal feedback at regular times during your employment.

DVD

Video 6

Watch this video showing a formal feedback session. As you watch, pay attention to several things:

- First, listen carefully to the supervisor's words. What were Ariel's strengths on the job? In what ways could Ariel improve her job performance?

- Also, notice the body language of both people. What does this suggest about their interaction?

In the spaces below, write down what the supervisor and employee said. When you have finished writing, watch the video again. Check to see how well you remembered their actual words.

" SUPERVISOR:_____

_____

_____

_____ "

" EMPLOYEE: _____

_____

_____

_____ "

" SUPERVISOR:_____

_____

_____

_____ "

The interaction in this video provides a good model to use when receiving feedback. Discuss as a class the lessons you can draw from this formal feedback session.

Giving Feedback

You are now prepared to receive feedback in the workplace. But part of your job may also involve giving feedback to others. This may include your co-workers and your supervisor. You can apply much of what you've learned about receiving feedback to the process of giving feedback.

First, you should always remain professional when giving feedback to others. Focus on the job performance and behaviors of the people you are evaluating. Don't allow personal feelings or opinions to affect your judgment. Remember to analyze such situations objectively. Consider the point of view of the employee you are evaluating when giving feedback.

Suppose your supervisor asks you to give feedback to your co-worker Michael. You and Michael both work as groundskeepers at a community park. Michael generally has a good attitude about doing routine maintenance and repairs around the park. However, he complains bitterly whenever you ask him to help clean up litter and garbage.

Try using the following script to give feedback to Michael:

I appreciate how you _____

_____ ,

but you need to improve _____

_____ .

Keep these same tips in mind when providing feedback to supervisors. However, also keep in mind your position relative to that of your supervisor's. It is important to treat your supervisor respectfully and professionally. For instance, a hospital employee might say to his or her supervisor, "It takes me longer to make my rounds because I think I need more training on the automatic blood pressure machine."

COMMUNICATION

The Real Story

As an employee, you may not have access to the same information that your supervisor does when he or she makes decisions. As a result, your supervisor may give you instructions that seem unfair. You might feel undeserved pressure or even disrespect. Your first instinct might be to get upset. Instead, try to gather missing information from your supervisor. This can help you to see the big picture and even learn to think like your supervisor. Read the exchange to the right, and consider how Armando gives feedback to his boss, the contractor.

1 CUSTOMER
"If you are not finished and out of my house in two days, I'm not going to pay you!"

2 OWNER OF CONTRACTING FIRM
"Jim, I need you to have your guys finish the job in two days."

4 TILE LAYER, ARMANDO
"I know we need to please the customer, but I do my best work when I have time to lay tile neatly and check the alignment."

3 CONTRACTOR, JIM
"Armando, I need you to finish laying the bathroom tile tonight."

What information could Jim, the contractor, have given Armando to help him better understand his request?
(Notice that Armando started with a positive statement, then added his constructive feedback.)

Now You Try It ...

Read the following scenario about Angela, the mechanic, and her boss, Clyde. Think about the information Clyde should share with Angela. Then answer the question below.

Clyde, the manager of an auto repair shop, gets a last-minute request from a local school district to repair some of their buses. Knowing this could lead to more work in the future, he asks one of his best mechanics, Angela, to work on her day off over the weekend.

Angela isn't happy about having to work on her day off. Clyde doesn't explain why he wants her to come in. Remember that Angela should always be respectful to Clyde but needs to know more information. What feedback should she give to Clyde?

_____

_____

_____

Pathways

Separating Feedback from Gossip

As an effective employee, you have the responsibility to seek accurate feedback from co-workers and supervisors you respect and trust. Feedback, especially when constructive, can help you improve your workplace performance and achieve professional and personal goals. Setting and achieving goals will boost your self-esteem. However, other comments may harm—rather than help—your ability to succeed.

Negative comments, such as gossip, in the workplace can lower your confidence and hurt your reputation. Whenever possible, avoid negative comments and instead focus on matters you can control, such as your career goals.

The following activities will help you better receive and manage co-workers' comments. After reading each activity, use the questions to start a group discussion, and evaluate how you would react in the same situation.

ACTIVITY

▶ **ACTIVITY 1: Office Gossip**

Sarah and Maleka do their usual huddle, complaining about co-workers as they walk by. Today, they have targeted one of their call center's most efficient and effective customer service representatives, Tanh. Every workplace has people like Sarah and Maleka. These office gossips tend to find doom and gloom in every situation unless they are the center of attention. Often, people who gossip about others have low self-esteem. In order to feel better about themselves, they instead seek to focus on and talk about the actions or shortcomings of others. In these conversations, they may also target people they see as threats to their own success.

Following are strategies that will help you avoid negativity in the workplace:

1. Avoid gossip. When people attempt to spread gossip, ignore them. Gossip won't travel far without an audience.

2. Do not compromise your own work. Focus on your goals—not negativity spread by gossipers.

3. If workplace gossip and demeaning comments continue, report it to your human resource representative or supervisor and ask for advice.

▶ **Self Reflection**

1. Have you ever been the subject of workplace gossip? If so, how did you react to it? How did others react to it?

_____

2. What was the outcome of your reaction?

_____

3. How might you change your behavior when confronted with gossiping co-workers in the future?

_____

PROBLEM SOLVING/CRITICAL THINKING

ACTIVITY

▶ ACTIVITY 2: Accepting Feedback

Sometimes co-workers, like supervisors, will give you feedback. By giving feedback, they're trying to help you perform better. Like you, they want what's best for the company. You should attempt to receive—and apply—feedback from others to improve your performance. Don't take feedback the wrong way. Use it to become the most effective employee you can be!

Read and discuss the script below. Then discuss the self-reflection questions.

▶ Self Reflection

1. Have you ever been in a situation like this? If so, how did you react to it?

2. What was the outcome of your reaction?

3. How would you change your behavior when given feedback by a co-worker in the future?

Answer the self-reflection questions, and use them as a basis to write what you learned about dealing with co-workers. Your instructor may ask volunteers to share their experiences with the class.

SHANNON: Hey Gina—do you have enough hangers for those shirts?

GINA: Hi, Shannon. I think I have enough. This shipment just came in and Shondra wants them hung up before I leave today.

SHANNON: I'm glad we're finally getting some fall clothes in stock. Remember that we need to organize and display the patterned shirts and then the solid colors. Do you need some help?

GINA: I didn't know we had to group the shirts that way! No one ever told me about color-coding. How come no one told me about this?

SHANNON: I'm sorry, I thought you knew about the display guidelines or else I would have helped you earlier.

GINA: I can't do my job right if I don't get the proper training.

SHANNON: I'm really sorry—I didn't mean to upset you. I'm just trying to help.

GINA: Well, thanks for your help. And I'm sorry, I didn't mean to be rude. I just get frustrated when I don't know all of the store policies.

SHANNON: No problem, Gina. If you ever have any questions about anything, please feel free to ask me. I'm here to help you in any way that I can. Now where did I put that color chart?

Performance Assessment

GOALS

EXAMINE the purpose and content of performance evaluations

ANALYZE common procedures for disciplinary action toward employees

LEARN terminology related to disciplinary action

TERMS

merit increase

cost-of-living increases

disciplinary action

It seemed like only yesterday that Suzanne Kahele began her job as a technician at a biology lab. Then her boss reminded her that the one-year anniversary of her employment was approaching. This meant it was time for her first annual performance review.

Like Suzanne, most employees receive formal reviews at regular intervals during their employment. Employers often use these official reports to make decisions about employees' positions and pay. For instance, Suzanne knew her employer would assess her, in part, based on her ability to run accurate tests. She also understood that earning an "exceeds expectations," rather than a simple "meets expectations" in this category could mean the difference between getting a raise or not.

Employees who receive excellent performance reviews are more likely to receive merit increases. A **merit increase** is a raise an employee earns because of outstanding performance. Employees who simply meet expectations might be more likely to receive cost-of-living increases. **Cost-of-living increases** are small raises designed to offset increasing prices of housing and consumer goods from one year to the next. You may not always receive a pay increase when you get a performance review. Sometimes companies cannot afford to give pay increases, even for employees with excellent performance reviews.

You have the right to speak out if you disagree with scores on your performance review. But you should remember to be calm and professional when doing so.

IN FOCUS: EMPLOYABILITY AND CAREER DEVELOPMENT

Performance Reviews

Effective employees should welcome performance reviews. They are one of many opportunities for you to receive feedback on your work. Supervisors take performance reviews very seriously because they are an official record.

Nothing you see on your performance review should come as a surprise. Responsible supervisors provide feedback to their direct-reports throughout the review period. Ideally, the formal review should reflect what you already know.

A performance review provides relevant information, such as the employee's name, title, and the time period covered by the review.

PERFORMANCE REVIEW

EMPLOYEE: Brandy Jackson
TITLE: Teacher Aide
REVIEW PERIOD: 2010–2011 Academic Year
DATE OF REVIEW: 6/7/11

JOB SKILLS: Brandy has shown a willingness to expand her job skills during this year. She has become an increasingly valuable member of our staff and has demonstrated a commitment to excellence that sets her apart from many of her peers.

WORK RESULTS: Brandy's work results are overall quite good. Many of the students she works with have shown improvement in their academic test scores. At times, she could better enforce classroom rules and prevent disruptive behavior among students.

COMMUNICATION: Brandy is a strong verbal communicator. She excels in speaking face-to-face with co-workers, students, and parents. In the next year, she could focus on bringing her written and electronic communication skills up to this same level.

These are the categories in which the employee will be evaluated.

Instead of numerical scores, this review provides descriptions of the employee's performance in each category.

PERFORMANCE EVALUATION

Employee:	Alejandro Gomez
Title:	Sales Associate
Review Period:	9/1/10 to 9/1/11
Date of Review:	9/8/11

This review lists the categories by which the employee will be evaluated.

This form uses numerical scores from 4 (excellent) to 1 (poor) to evaluate an employee.

	4 EXCELLENT	3 GOOD	2 AVERAGE	1 POOR
Quality of Work		X		
Dependability		X		
Punctuality			X	
Teamwork	X			
Initiative	X			
Communication			X	
Job Knowledge		X		

Procedures for Disciplinary Action

Disciplinary action is used to correct employee behavior that violates workplace rules. Have you heard the expression "written up?" This refers to a written report that details disciplinary action taken against an employee.

The human resources department usually helps carry out disciplinary actions. Remember that employers have these procedures to help you grow and improve. If you don't change problem behaviors, you could lose your job.

STEP BY STEP

This flowchart shows how disciplinary action might progress at a company. This process is usually outlined in a corporate policy manual.

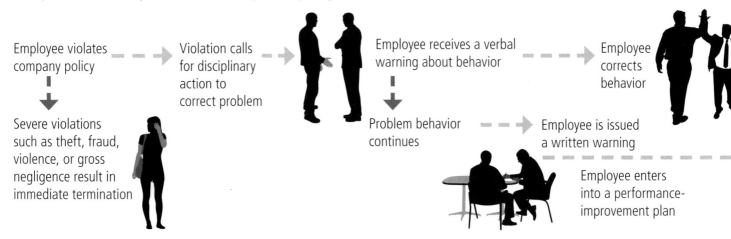

Employee violates company policy

Violation calls for disciplinary action to correct problem

Employee receives a verbal warning about behavior

Employee corrects behavior

Severe violations such as theft, fraud, violence, or gross negligence result in immediate termination

Problem behavior continues

Employee is issued a written warning

Employee enters into a performance-improvement plan

ACTIVITY

▶ **Know the Terminology**

Read the words and definitions in the table to the right. Then demonstrate your understanding of these terms by writing four statements or questions related to the terms on the lines below.

Example: *Florida is an employment-at-will state.*

_____

_____

_____

_____

_____

_____

_____

_____

DISCIPLINE-RELATED TERMS

Term	Definition
Employment at will	Employment in which a company can terminate an employee at any time without providing a cause
Excessive absences	Missing work beyond the number of days allowed by company policy
Fraud	Deceitful or dishonest behavior; may also be illegal
Gross negligence	Extreme or intentional failure to complete one's duties
Insubordination	Disrespect or disobedience to people in positions of authority
Negligence	Failure to complete one's duties
Tardiness	Lateness; arriving after the proper time
Termination	The ending of employment; firing
Theft	Taking property from its rightful owner
Violence	Use of physical force in order to hurt or intimidate another person

ETHICS AND LEGAL RESPONSIBILITIES

Right-to-Work States

In Right-to-Work states, people can work at companies that have unions without being required to join these unions. This exclusion does not apply to people who work for airlines or railways.

If your job requires or offers union membership, learn all that you can about it so you can make an informed decision.

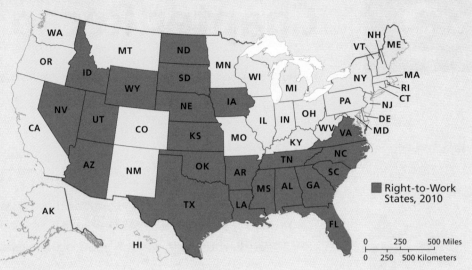

Right-to-Work States, 2010

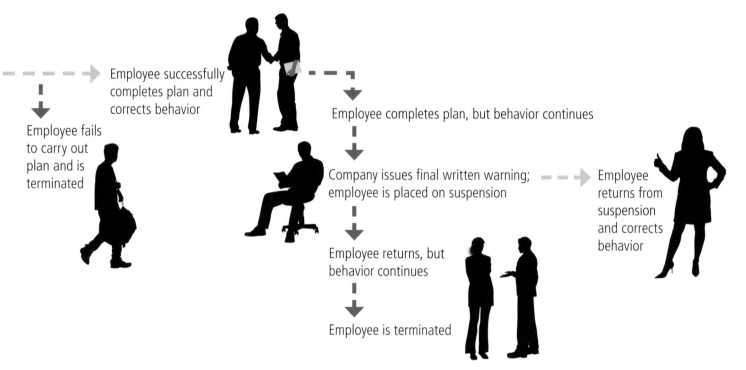

Employee successfully completes plan and corrects behavior

Employee fails to carry out plan and is terminated

Employee completes plan, but behavior continues

Company issues final written warning; employee is placed on suspension

Employee returns, but behavior continues

Employee returns from suspension and corrects behavior

Employee is terminated

COMMUNICATION

Fair or Unfair?

During your career, you may receive a performance evaluation or disciplinary action that you believe to be unfair. If so, take time to review the situation. Think honestly about the disciplinary action or evaluation. Move past your initial hurt feelings. If you still believe that your supervisor treated you unfairly, you can take steps to correct the problem. If you are a member of a union, there may be established rules and guidelines that you will need to follow. Your union contract should explain this process.

If you are not in a union, consider first putting into writing why you think the evaluation or disciplinary action was unfair. Use facts to back up your statements. Avoid using emotional or confrontational language. Then ask to present this document to your supervisor. Set up a meeting so you can discuss the issues you raise. If your supervisor seems unwilling to help, consult your company's policy manual. This manual should explain how to raise your concerns to human resources or another authority in the company.

Chapter Recap

Using the list below, place a checkmark next to the goals you achieved in Chapter 3.

▶ **In Lesson 1, you . . .**

- ❏ Learned how self-esteem can affect your work
- ❏ Wrote about your personal and professional accomplishments that build your self-esteem
- ❏ Studied techniques for building self-esteem in the workplace

▶ **In Lesson 2, you . . .**

- ❏ Examined the purposes of feedback in the workplace
- ❏ Applied strategies for handling feedback and improving your performance
- ❏ Learned how to give constructive feedback

▶ **In Lesson 3, you . . .**

- ❏ Examined the purpose and content of performance evaluations
- ❏ Analyzed common procedures for disciplinary action toward employees
- ❏ Learned terminology related to disciplinary action

Chapter Review

Name: _____ Date: _____

▶ **Directions:** Choose the best answer.

1. Employers show that they value their employees by

   A. investing money in training them.
   B. offering employment at will.
   C. looking for ways to discipline employees unfairly.

2. When receiving feedback in the workplace, you should

   A. avoid asking questions of your supervisor while receiving feedback.
   B. take notes in order to remember details of feedback you receive.
   C. focus only on negative feedback so that you may make improvements.

3. When giving feedback in the workplace, you should

   A. consider your personal feelings toward co-workers when making judgments.
   B. handle it casually to prevent co-workers from taking it too seriously.
   C. remain objective about the performance and behavior of your co-workers.

▶ **Directions:** Determine whether the following statements are true or false. If the statement is true, write T. If the statement is false, write F. Then rewrite the false statement to make it true.

4. You can build self-esteem in the workplace by setting daily goals for yourself.

   _____

   _____

5. Formal performance reviews have little impact on employee wages or salaries.

   _____

   _____

▶ **Directions:** Write your answer to the question on the lines below.

6. What are some important tips to remember when giving feedback to a supervisor?

   _____

   _____

   _____

   _____

CHAPTER 3

Complete a Self-Evaluation

▶ At times, an employer may ask you to complete a self-evaluation to analyze your performance. Employers may use this along with your annual performance evaluation—written by your supervisor—to make a decision regarding any potential pay increase.

7. The form to the right shows what a typical self-evaluation might look like.

- Complete this form based on your performance in this class.

- Think of your classroom tasks as though they were workplace assignments.

- Reflect on whether you would deserve a pay increase based on the results of your self-evaluation.

EMPLOYEE SELF-EVALUATION

Employee:

Title:

Date:

Supervisor:

	4 Outstanding	3 Good	2 Fair	1 Poor
Punctuality				
Attendance				
Work Ethic				
Completion of Assigned Tasks				

What do you feel are your best accomplishments to date?

_____

_____

In what areas would you like to improve?

_____

_____

What are your goals going forward?

_____

_____

Name: _____ Date: _____

Put Steps in Sequence

▶ For this activity, suppose that an employee has demonstrated a pattern of arriving late to work. The statements below describe the steps of a company's disciplinary action toward this employee.

8. Place these steps in the proper sequence by numbering them from 1 to 8 on the lines next to each step.

_____ The employee's lateness continues. The manager schedules a formal feedback session to discuss why this behavior has not been corrected.

_____ The company places the employee on suspension. He receives a final written warning. This warning indicates that further lateness will result in termination.

_____ Along with a written warning, the company issues a performance improvement plan to the employee.

_____ The employee returns from suspension. After a week back on the job, he again arrives late for work.

_____ The employee completes the performance improvement plan, but he continues to arrive late for work.

_____ A manager holds an informal feedback session to discuss the employee's lateness.

_____ The company terminates the employee due to continued lateness.

_____ Because the lateness continues in the wake of formal feedback, the company issues a written warning to the employee.

Chapter Review

Develop a Plan of Action

▶ Suppose you work as a restaurant manager. One employee, Tashawnah, provides great customer service and is always friendly toward her co-workers. However, several nights a week, some of Tashawnah's friends come into the restaurant. They hang out until the restaurant closes for the night.

Tashawnah's friends always purchase food. But they often linger at the counter and distract Tashawnah from her duties. When she cleans the dining room, Tashawnah usually spends much of her time wiping the tables near her friends.

Overall, Tashawnah is a good employee. But you recognize that the situation with her friends is a problem. Complete the performance plan below to help Tashawnah focus more on her work and less on her friends.

EMPLOYEE PERFORMANCE PLAN

9. What is the nature of the problem?

_____

10. What behaviors does the employee exhibit that negatively affect the workplace?

_____

11. What steps should the employee take to change this behavior?

_____

_____

12. What is the desired outcome?

_____

13. When should these changes be made? Should deadlines or follow-up meetings be scheduled?

_____

The Diverse Workplace

TERMS

diverse

gender

cultural sensitivity

When you become an employee, you join a team of co-workers. This team could include just a few people or a large group of employees. No matter its size, everyone on this team should be working toward the same purpose.

Though you may all be united in working toward a common goal, this doesn't mean that your co-workers will all be the same. In fact, most workplaces are diverse. If something is **diverse**, this means that it is made up of many different parts or characteristics. A diverse workplace includes people of different beliefs, ages, genders, and backgrounds. **Gender** refers to a person's sex, either male or female.

All jobs are open to employees from different races and ethnic backgrounds. As workplaces become more diverse, it becomes increasingly important that employees learn to work well with people of different backgrounds. The people you encounter in the workplace may be very different than the people you socialize with. They may be considerably older than you or of another race. However, if all employees act professionally, they can work together to get the job done. The bar graph below illustrates that diversity exists, to varying degrees, in many different career fields.

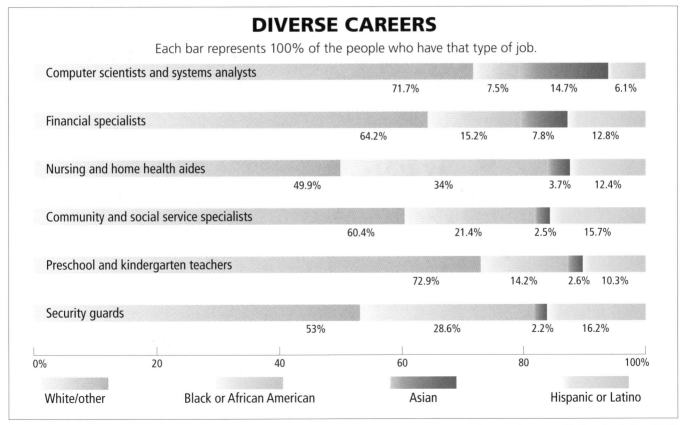

DIVERSE CAREERS

Each bar represents 100% of the people who have that type of job.

Job	White/other	Black or African American	Asian	Hispanic or Latino
Computer scientists and systems analysts	71.7%	7.5%	14.7%	6.1%
Financial specialists	64.2%	15.2%	7.8%	12.8%
Nursing and home health aides	49.9%	34%	3.7%	12.4%
Community and social service specialists	60.4%	21.4%	2.5%	15.7%
Preschool and kindergarten teachers	72.9%	14.2%	2.6%	10.3%
Security guards	53%	28.6%	2.2%	16.2%

0%   20   40   60   80   100%

White/other   Black or African American   Asian   Hispanic or Latino

Source: Bureau of Labor Statistics, 2009

Cultural Sensitivity

When working in a diverse workplace, you should always try to demonstrate cultural sensitivity. **Cultural sensitivity** is an awareness of differences between cultures. It means being sensitive to the fact that these differences can affect people's ideas and behaviors.

Cultural sensitivity calls for employees to be tolerant of one another's differences. Companies may offer employees instruction on how to demonstrate this in the workplace. For instance, your employer might provide you with a list of words or behaviors to avoid saying or doing, such as:

- asking a co-worker, "Why are you wearing that on your head?"

- sending e-mail messages that include jokes about groups of people

- laughing at or making fun of unfamiliar behaviors or actions by co-workers

A good general rule for showing cultural sensitivity is to carefully watch what you say and do in the workplace. At times, you might say or do something simply out of curiosity. However, your words or actions could still be seen as offensive.

COMMUNICATION

Change the Subject

There are many steps that you can take to respect diversity in the workplace. But you can't control what your co-workers say and do. If a co-worker brings up an inappropriate topic, you should try to change the subject. Think of safe topics, like traffic or the weather which won't offend others. Ignoring an offensive remark and quickly changing the subject sends a clear message to a co-worker. A good rule of thumb is that if a subject is not work related, it probably shouldn't be discussed.

Some sensitivity issues relate to characteristics that might not be obvious. These could include sexual preference, religion, or political beliefs. If something could be seen as offensive, it's best to not say or do it.

At times, you may be asked a culturally insensitive question. If this happens, feel free to decline to answer the question or try to change the subject. Or you may decide to answer the question and explain why it was inappropriate.

 To learn more about resolving conflicts, see Appendix A.

ACTIVITY

▶ Working Together

Think about some of your previous work or volunteer experiences. In particular, consider those times in which you worked with a person or group of people that was different from you. Use your recollections of these experiences to answer the questions below.

1. How did the culture or background of the person or group differ from your own?

_____

_____

2. What steps did you take to work successfully with this person or group?

_____

_____

Successful employees are professional. Behaving professionally means being culturally sensitive.

Discrimination

Companies work to promote diversity in the workplace. One way they do this is by issuing discrimination policies. Discrimination is the unfair treatment of people based on a characteristic other than merit. Some types of discrimination can be easy to spot. These include discrimination based on:

- age
- gender
- race
- ethnicity

However, other types of discrimination may not be as obvious. For instance, some people might discriminate against others based on:

- religious beliefs
- political beliefs
- socioeconomic class

In addition to company policies, federal laws also protect employees from discrimination. The Civil Rights Act of 1964 prohibits discrimination on the basis of gender, race, ethnicity, religion, or natural origin. The Equal Employment Opportunity Commission (EEOC) was created in a provision of the Civil Rights Act to enforce the law.

If the men in this office exclude Kelly because she is a woman, they are guilty of gender discrimination.

The Equal Pay Act of 1963 makes it illegal for companies to pay men and women different salaries for the same work. Other statutes protect against discrimination because of age or disabilities.

Both federal laws and company policies offer employees ways to speak out against discrimination. If you believe you're being discriminated against, consult these to learn about ways to correct the problem.

Examine the workplace scenarios on page 89. They will explain ways in which discrimination may happen in the workplace.

CHARGES OF EMPLOYER DISCRIMINATION IN THE U.S.

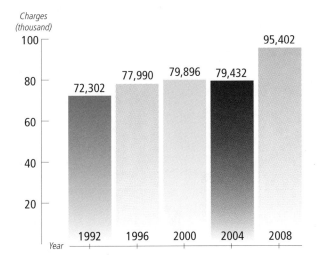

Charges (thousand)

Year	Charges
1992	72,302
1996	77,990
2000	79,896
2004	79,432
2008	95,402

This graph shows the total number of individual discrimination charges filed by employees. The individual charges may include several types of discrimination.

TYPES OF EMPLOYEE DISCRIMINATION CHARGES

TYPE	NUMBER OF CHARGES	% OF TOTAL CHARGES
Retaliation—all types	36,258	36.3%
Race	35,890	35.9%
Gender	29,029	29.1%
Disability	25,165	25.2%
Age	23,264	23.3%
National origin	11,304	11.3%
Religion	3,790	3.8%

This table lists the most common types of employer discrimination reported by employees, who often claim to be victims of several types of discrimination.

Source: U.S. Equal Employment Opportunity Commission

EXAMPLES OF DISCRIMINATION

1 A male supervisor will only issue important assignments to male employees. He assigns female employees small or unimportant tasks. He is discriminating against female employees based on gender.

3 A manager always gives extra shifts to employees who attend the same church that he does. This is an example of discrimination because of religious affiliation. This manager is treating other employees unfairly. Because they do not attend his church, they are not getting the same opportunities as the employees who do.

2 A white supervisor rarely communicates with her Hispanic male subordinate. She believes that she can't "connect" with him. Because of this, she simply doesn't check in with him. This leaves him out of the loop on many important pieces of information around the workplace. The supervisor's actions are discriminatory based on ethnic background.

4 An older worker is routinely left out of important meetings by his co-workers. These workers are discriminating against him because of age.

ACTIVITY

▶ **Discrimination Policy**

Read the sample employer discrimination policy to the right. Then answer the questions below, either in a class discussion or on a separate sheet of paper.

1. What do you think it means when this company states that it is an "equal opportunity employer"?

2. Would a manager in this company be permitted to promote an employee based on his or her race?

3. What characteristics are employees of this company forbidden to use as a basis for discrimination?

Anti-Discrimination Policy

Well-Being Medical Systems (WBMS) is an equal opportunity employer. WBMS will not discriminate and will take action to prevent discrimination in all areas of operations, including employment, recruiting, promotions, payment, and termination. Discrimination against any employee or prospective employee on the basis of race, ethnicity, religion, sexual preference, or gender will not be tolerated.

Harassment

You've learned that many employers have discrimination policies. These employers also have policies aimed at preventing harassment. Harassment is any kind of bothersome, demeaning, irritating, or annoying behavior. When this behavior is of a sexual nature, it is called sexual harassment. The Civil Rights Act of 1964 protects employees from sexual harassment in the workplace.

Harassment includes a wide range of behaviors. Threatening or bullying a co-worker could be considered harassment. Acting hostile toward a co-worker based on a personal trait, such as weight or a stutter, would also qualify as harassment.

Harassing behaviors also extend to workplace communication. Suppose you told an offensive joke about a group of people. Or perhaps you pulled a prank that targeted an employee because of a personal trait. These both would likely violate your employer's harassment policy. Similarly, sharing magazines or Web sites with offensive content could also be harassment.

It's important to remember that a workplace usually includes people of many different backgrounds. Diversity may lead people to interpret others' actions differently. A comment or an act may seem like harmless behavior to you. But it might be viewed as harassment by people of a different age, ethnicity, or gender.

HARASSMENT CHARGES RECEIVED BY U.S. EQUAL EMPLOYMENT OPPORTUNITY COMMISSION & FAIR EMPLOYMENT PRACTICES AGENCIES

Charges Received (thousand)

Year	Charges
1992	15,200
1996	20,986
2000	24,239
2004	22,910
2008	32,535

Source: U.S. Equal Employment Opportunity Commission

The national Equal Employment Opportunity Commission works with various local and state agencies to resolve allegations of harassment in the workplace.

As an employee, it's crucial that you recognize and understand harassment so that you may avoid it. When it comes to harassment, intent doesn't matter. The only thing that does is the way your behavior affects another person. In other words, ignorance—or a lack of understanding of the consequences of your behavior—is no excuse.

Examine the workplace scenarios on page 91. They will demonstrate ways in which harassment may happen in the workplace.

Touching a co-worker in any way can be seen as harassment. You may be comfortable putting your hand on a friend's arm or around a family member's shoulders. But these seemingly friendly actions may make co-workers uncomfortable.

EXAMPLES OF HARASSMENT

1 An employee posts a printout of a joke that he finds funny. However, the joke makes fun of women. Several of the employee's co-workers are women. This type of communication represents harassment in the workplace.

3 A female employee asks a male employee to show his abs to her. Sometimes a comment like this is meant to be funny. But it can be interpreted as offensive. Some behaviors may seem appropriate among your social group, but they may not be appropriate in the workplace.

2 A male employee asks a female co-worker to go on a date with him. She turns him down. He continues to ask her to go out and also sends her flowers at work. Even if he does not threaten her, his pushy behavior makes the female co-worker uncomfortable. Therefore, it's sexual harassment.

4 A group of employees of one race threatens an employee of another race. The group threatens to damage the employee's car. This type of hostile behavior clearly constitutes harassment.

ACTIVITY

▶ **Harassment Policy**

Read the sample employer harassment policy to the right. Then answer the questions below, either in a class discussion or on a separate sheet of paper.

1. How would you describe this company's attitude toward harassment?

2. What are some of the ways that this company can address harassment in the workplace?

3. What factors might this company take into consideration when dealing with a harassment complaint?

Harassment Policy

Harassment will be dealt with appropriately. The Smith Company will deal with complaints of harassment based on what it believes to be appropriate under the circumstances. For example, this may include training, referral to counseling and/or disciplinary action, withholding of a promotion or pay increase, reassignment, suspension, or termination of employment.

Where Are You Going?

GOALS

TERMS

promoted

corporate structure

pay grade

notice

Demetrius Rogers had been working as a clerk at a shipping store for several months. In that time, he'd quickly learned the basic skills required for his job. He now felt very comfortable with his daily responsibilities. In fact, he'd begun to seek out other duties to perform around the store. As he observed his manager at work, he decided that he would like to be promoted to the position of manager. A worker is **promoted** when he or she is advanced to a higher-ranking position.

As an employee, you may share Demetrius's ambitions. One of the first steps toward earning a promotion is to understand your place in your company. To do this, you must look at the company's corporate structure. A **corporate structure** is the way in which a company's jobs and departments are organized. By understanding corporate structure, you can identify positions to which you might advance. On the other hand, you might also recognize that your opportunities are limited. In these cases, you may decide to pursue additional training or a job with another business. Examine the two charts shown below. They display the corporate structures of a retail company and a medical laboratory.

A salesperson in this retail company could advance to become Retail Operations Manager.

To advance in this laboratory, a technician would need to earn a bachelor's degree.

Corporate Board of Directors

- Merchandising Director
  - Purchasers
- Retail Operations Manager
  - Store Manager
    - Area Sales Manager
      - Salespeople
- Financial Director
  - Accounting Manager
    - Accountants
  - Inventory Controller
    - Inventory Staff
- Marketing Director
  - Advertising and Public Relations Staff

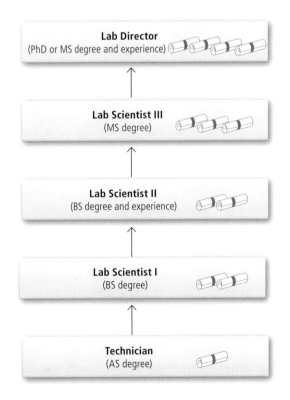

Lab Director
(PhD or MS degree and experience)

↑

Lab Scientist III
(MS degree)

↑

Lab Scientist II
(BS degree and experience)

↑

Lab Scientist I
(BS degree)

↑

Technician
(AS degree)

To learn more about training, certifications, and degrees, see Appendix B.

ACTIVITY

▶ ## What Are Your Goals?

In the space below, write both short- and long-term goals. As you consider these, try to match your personal goals with workplace goals. For instance, suppose you want to buy a car. Think about how much money you would need to earn to pay for it. This information would likely affect your career goals.

3 MONTHS: Personal

_____

3 MONTHS: Workplace

_____

1 YEAR: Personal

_____

1 YEAR: Workplace

_____

5 YEARS: Personal

_____

5 YEARS: Workplace

_____

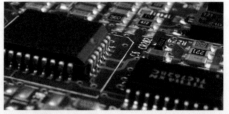

Finish my A+ certification in computer repair

Receive promotion to shift supervisor

Earn my bachelor's degree

PROBLEM SOLVING/CRITICAL THINKING

Balancing Work and Life

All employees find themselves trying to balance their work responsibilities with their everyday lives. Despite your best efforts, you may sometimes find that personal circumstances prevent you from reaching a career goal. This could be a promotion, a raise, or some other milestone. Perhaps your lack of transportation means you sometimes show up late for work. Or maybe your childcare duties don't allow you to work a flexible schedule.

It's important to remember that these issues may only be temporary. For instance, suppose childcare needs affect the amount of hours you can work. Think ahead to when your kids would start school. At that point, your childcare responsibilities may no longer be as much of an issue.

Try to take a long view when thinking of your career goals. This way, you may plan ahead to receive extra training or earn a degree. The solutions may not happen immediately. If you stay positive and focused, you can reach your career goals.

Promotion Plan

Now that you've made both short- and long-term goals, it's time to create a plan for promotion. In some cases, a promotion requires additional education. You will learn more about furthering your education in Lesson 3. In other cases, an employee must show mastery of current duties to earn a promotion, receive a pay increase, or reach a certain pay grade.

A **pay grade** is a certain level of payment that an employee can reach for the work they perform. For example, an employee might want to reach a pay grade of at least $40,000 per year. Whatever your goals may be, the steps in the flowchart below provide tips that you can use to create your own promotion plan.

STEPS TO EARN A PROMOTION

1 Begin to work toward a promotion as soon as you start a new job. Ask your manager or a mentor about the skills you need to advance in the company.

3 Regularly monitor your progress. Look objectively at the steps you've taken. Don't be too hard on yourself, and keep working to achieve your goals.

4 Look and act the part of a successful employee. Being professional will help you gain a positive reputation in the workplace. Companies promote employees who are competent, dependable, and trustworthy.

5 Volunteer for additional responsibilities. Doing so will show your dedication and showcase your ability to handle multiple tasks at once. Also, taking on extra responsibilities proves your value to the company.

6 Develop relationships with mentors. A mentor can help spread positive feedback about your work at higher levels of the company. You can also benefit from a mentor's own experiences about being promoted.

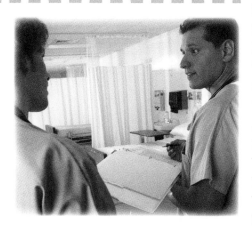

2 Set goals to develop additional skills. You should prioritize skills that need the most improvement. As you go about your work, take advantage of opportunities to learn and practice these skills.

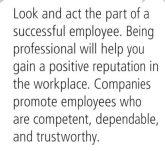

7 Develop a good relationship with your boss. Take opportunities to showcase your skills. Use your job performance to win over your supervisor.

9 Most importantly, produce results. Record evidence of your excellent performance. Sharing these positive results allows you to make a strong case for promotion.

8 Effective employees should be team players. The ability to work as part of a team often proves crucial to receiving a raise or a new position.

PLAY VIDEO

I Deserve A Raise! When asking for a raise, remember to list specific reasons for why you deserve it. For instance, you could say, "I consistently beat my sales goals" or "I managed the merchandise move to the second floor." Avoid using generalities such as, "I work really hard." The better the information you provide, the better your chances are of getting the raise you want.

Video 7

Watch the video of two employees asking for raises. Then answer the questions that follow.

1. Which employee's request for a raise do you find more effective? Why?

_____

_____

2. Why is the other employee's request less effective?

_____

_____

When you have finished watching the video, perform the same scenario with a classmate. Take turns being the employee asking for a raise and the supervisor listening to the request.

Moving On

At some point during the course of your career, you may realize that your next step is to change jobs. Perhaps you can't advance any further in your company. You may have gained the experience you need to apply for a better job somewhere else. No matter what your reason for leaving, it's important to approach this process the right way.

Before you leave, research your employer's policies about any payments and benefits you are owed. Work with your supervisor or human resources representative to determine what to do about any sick or vacation time you've earned. You should also ask about your health benefits. You may not be covered by your new employer's healthcare plan right away. If you have a delay in coverage, you can continue your existing health benefits through a program called COBRA. This program allows employees to keep temporarily the health coverage from their former employer when between jobs or until they join a new plan. Although expensive, COBRA plans allow for continuing coverage without interruption.

Remember to write down your supervisor's and human resource manager's name and contact information. You may need this information for your resume or a future job application.

COMMUNICATION

Saying Goodbye

Leaving a job is never easy. However, it can be made much easier by behaving professionally as you prepare to leave.

First, you should always give your employer notice that you intend to leave. **Notice** is a warning or announcement that an employee is leaving. In most cases, people try to give two weeks of notice.

After giving notice, you should also write a letter of resignation. This letter should explain the details of your departure, such as pursuing an opportunity in another field. Keep it short and simple. Don't try to explain your reasons for leaving. But you should thank your employer for the opportunities and experiences you had on the job. Try to maintain a positive relationship with your employer. This may help you when seeking a reference in the future. You may even wish to ask your supervisor to serve as a reference before you leave.

As you did during your employment, remain professional while leaving your job. Don't burn bridges with your co-workers. You never know when you might encounter them again.

A Better You

GOALS

LEARN the types of training, certification, and degrees you need to reach your career goals 97

STUDY the ways employers help employees learn new skills 98

APPLY what you've learned to update your resume 99

TERMS

LLC

CPR/AED

Effective employees are constantly learning and developing new skills on the job. However, many employees also need additional training, certification, or degrees in order to reach their career goals. Perhaps you already have a degree or certification in a particular field. It's possible that you may need to seek continuing education or professional development to keep or earn a promotion at your job.

For example, some childcare workers must attend a certain number of hours of continuing development courses. This allows them to keep their certification from year to year. Many childcare workers must also become certified in first aid. In some cases, an employer may pay for or help employees pay for these types of programs. In other instances, employees must pay their own way. Study the diagram below to see one example of how these requirements affect a particular field.

CONTINUING EDUCATION = SUCCESS

A Paloma is a medical records technician. She has an AAS degree in Health Information Technology.

F Paloma continues her education by taking management training classes.

B Paloma works to earn her Registered Health Information Technician (RHIT) credential.

E Paloma earns a BS in Computer Information Systems and becomes a health information manager.

C Paloma takes classes to specialize in cancer registry.

D Paloma wants to stay current in her profession, so she takes advanced computer classes.

 To learn more about training, certifications, and degrees, see Appendix B.

ACTIVITY

▶ ## How to Achieve Your Goals

Review the five-year goals you set for yourself in Lesson 2. As you recall these goals, determine the types of training, certification, degrees, or ongoing learning you need to achieve them.

The three examples below show certain career goals and the steps that employees would need to take in order to reach them. Refer to these as a guide for your own planning.

Jennifer wants to establish a cake decorating business.

- She decides to work from her house and begins to find customers.

- She investigates types of government funding available to women who want to start a small business.

- She decides to create an **LLC (limited liability company)** to protect her personal finances against the risks of starting a business.

Maylea works as a dental assistant but wants to become a dental hygienist.

- She first needs to attend an accredited dental hygiene school.

- She begins working a flexible schedule so she can go to school and work at the same time.

- She will have to obtain at least a certificate or associate's degree in dental hygiene.

- She then must pass a licensing exam in her home state.

DeSean has decided that he wants to change careers and become a police officer.

- He researches the job requirements of his local police department and decides to take a course in law enforcement.

- He looks online and finds an appropriate course at his local community college.

- He signs up for a gym membership since police officers need to be in top physical condition.

- DeSean learns that many police departments are seeking officers that speak a second language, so he signs up for a Spanish class.

After you have identified the steps needed to reach your career goals, use the Internet to conduct additional research.

- Determine where in your local area to find additional training.

- Determine how long these steps might take, and how much they might cost.

- Use this information to reexamine your goals. Then make a 10-year career goal.

Notes: _____

_____

_____

10-YEAR GOAL:

_____

_____

Employer Assistance

Many employers encourage their employees to take steps to improve their workplace skills. When employees better themselves, they also strengthen their company's workforce. Employers support these improvement efforts in various ways.

Some employers will provide training directly to their employees. Companies may also assist employees pursuing new degrees or certifications by helping to pay tuition. They may provide flexibility in work schedules so employees can attend classes. Finally, employers can sponsor outside training for their employees. This training might include learning about new equipment or safety procedures, or enhancing management skills.

Remember that you can gain skills and experience from every job you hold. Take advantage of any opportunities to learn new skills. These are especially valuable when your employer provides them at no cost. You should also consider volunteering to lead projects or organizations in your workplace. Those experiences can help you to improve your leadership skills.

▶ First Aid and CPR/AED Certification

Some employers offer first aid and CPR/AED certification. **CPR/AED** (cardiopulmonary resuscitation and automated external defibrillator) training teaches employees life-saving procedures.

▶ Professional Development

Many employees seek professional development training to become familiar with the latest techniques, equipment, or policies. They use training to keep up with changes in their jobs. For example, graphic artists should continually become certified and experienced in using the newest types of computer software. Many employers will pay for this training for their regular, full-time employees.

▶ Tuition Assistance

At times, employees may choose to take courses or seminars on their own. Often, an employee's continuing education will relate to his or her current job. In these cases, employers may pay some or all of the cost. As with professional development, companies providing such assistance expect to receive a more knowledgeable employee in return.

Technology changes quickly. Continuing education is the best way to remain up to date.

IN FOCUS: EMPLOYABILITY AND CAREER DEVELOPMENT

Your "Current" Resume

The resume you created while looking for a job should not stay the same for long. Every month or so, review any new certifications, skills, training, or leadership opportunities you've gained from your job. You will find it much easier to update your resume as you go rather than after a period of several years.

The graphic below provides examples of how to take new skills, training, and experiences, and properly describe them on your resume. You should also note where this information is placed.

 A

I was in charge of a group that figured out which new software to buy.

List this skill under **Experience**. Leadership and analysis skills are useful for any job.

 B

I got my associate's degree so I could be a Web designer.

Place this information under **Education**. Make sure that you correctly identify and describe the degrees or certifications you receive.

 C

I know how to use a lot of computer design programs.

List this achievement under **Skills/Certifications**. Here you can showcase skills that may not directly relate to your work experience.

Kianna A. Brooks

18930 68th Ave NE, Apt. 1107
Kenmore, WA 98028-2663
(425) 545-5555
brooks_ka@pax.com

Summary of Qualifications
Experienced computer support specialist skilled in diagnosing and resolving a variety of problems associated with computer hardware and software.

Experience
Computer Support Assistant, September 2010 to Present
WaterSource, Inc., Bothell, WA
- Resolve employee problems and questions related to company computer systems
- **A** **Led a research group that analyzed and purchased software for the company**
- Monitor performance of company networks and resolve technical issues that arise

Volunteer Help-Desk Technician, June 2010 to September 2010
Specialty Products, Inc., Kenmore, WA
- Responded to customer calls and e-mails requesting assistance using company website
- Determined problems and provided step-by-step instructions to help customers resolve issues

Education
B **Cascadia Community College**, Bothell, WA
Associate Degree in Applied Science—
Web Application Programming Technology (May 2012)

Lynnwood High School, Lynnwood, WA
- High school diploma (June 2007)

Skills/Certifications
Specialized at troubleshooting local area network (LAN) and wide area network (WAN) problems
 C **Proficient with Adobe® Photoshop®, Acrobat®, and Illustrator®**

Pathwavs

Me in Ten Years. . .

Even though it was tiring for Brandon to work during the day and take classes at night, he never took his eye off the prize. Brandon wants to become a forensic scientist. One day, he hopes to specialize in firearms and tool marks. These experts examine crime scene evidence such as guns, fired and unfired bullets, and gunshot residue. They also identify tools used in a crime, such as those used for forcing open windows or doors.

Brandon had to leave college and get a full-time job when his girlfriend had a baby. Today he's back in school, attending part-time evening classes to pursue his dream.

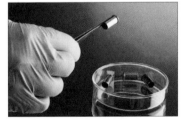

CRIME SCENE INVESTIGATOR

Currently, Brandon attends community college to earn his Associate in Science (AS) degree in crime scene technology. This will allow Brandon to gain work experience in his desired field. He will also earn more money than at his current retail job. Brandon can use this extra money to pay for part of his tuition for Bachelor of Science (BS) degree classes that he'll need to become a forensic scientist.

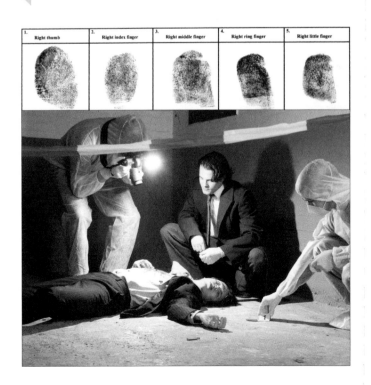

COMMUNICATION

Read Brandon's 10-year plan. Then complete your own 10-year plan in the table that follows. You will not have room for one goal per year, so plan carefully.

BRANDON IN 10 YEARS

Year	Goal	Investment
1	Brandon will finish his general education classes for his Associate of Science (AS) degree	Attending classes: free time, money
2	Brandon works as an intern for his local police department's CSI unit	Working as intern: free time
3	Brandon works as an intern for the Bureau of Alcohol, Tobacco, and Firearms	Working as intern: free time
4	Brandon earns his AS degree and lands a job as a crime scene investigator	Finishing degree: free time, money Finding job: free time
6	Brandon begins taking night classes to earn his Bachelor of Science (BS) degree in forensic science	Attending classes: free time, money
9	Brandon completes his BS degree in forensic science and lands a job with a private forensics laboratory	Finishing degree: free time, money Finding job: free time
10	Brandon becomes a certified firearms and toolmark examiner	Becoming certified: free time, completion of written and practical examinations

ME IN 10 YEARS

Year	Goal	Investment

Present Your Plan

Using the information in your 10-year plan, create and deliver a multimedia slide presentation, such as a PowerPoint, to your class. If you are unfamiliar with such software, use an online tutorial to get up to speed. Your presentation should include slides outlining your planned progress. You also should include at least one chart or graph and one photograph. Use the following guidelines to prepare your report:

- Use informational texts, Web sites, and/or technical materials to review and apply information relating to your chosen career field.

- Create a table, chart, or other graphic figure to support the information in your presentation.

- Make sure your sources are reliable by using mostly *.gov*, *.org*, or *.edu* Web sites.

- Remember that your audience includes your fellow work-readiness students. Make sure to deliver your report in a professional and businesslike manner.

The use of photographs helps show your audience the different duties that someone with your desired career must do.

The following slides are examples from a presentation that Brandon might give. You should model your slides after these examples.

You can easily use data from the government or an organization to populate a graph for a multimedia slide. This graph shows projected employment data through 2018.

Make sure to provide sources for information that you present.

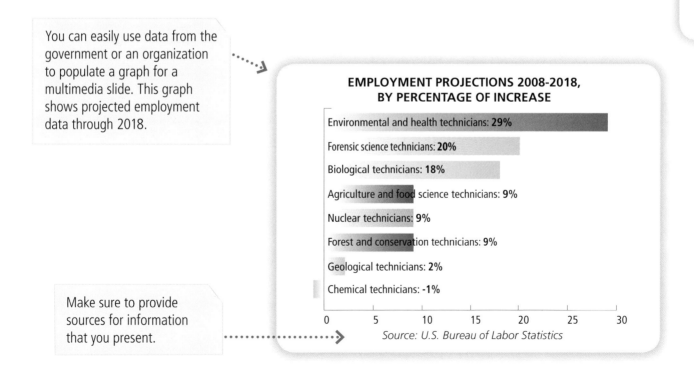

EMPLOYMENT PROJECTIONS 2008-2018, BY PERCENTAGE OF INCREASE

Environmental and health technicians: **29%**
Forensic science technicians: **20%**
Biological technicians: **18%**
Agriculture and food science technicians: **9%**
Nuclear technicians: **9%**
Forest and conservation technicians: **9%**
Geological technicians: **2%**
Chemical technicians: **-1%**

0   5   10   15   20   25   30

Source: U.S. Bureau of Labor Statistics

When figuring costs and benefits, don't think only of financial ones. Pursuing additional education also means additional time and effort. However, the benefits of continuing education also include higher self-esteem and a sense of achievement.

Costs and Benefits

Associate of Science degree—Crime Scene Technology

- **Costs**: $22,700; time away from family
- **Benefits**: Salary $32,000+; sense of accomplishment; employment as a professional

Bachelor of Science degree—Forensic Science

- **Costs**: $24,800; time away from family; schoolwork in addition to demanding full-time job
- **Benefits**: Salary $55,000+; sense of achievement; professional occupation; higher self-esteem

Certification in Firearms and Tool Marks

- **Costs**: $250 for fees; time to study for certification exams
- **Benefits**: AFTE certification; recognition of expert status; achievement of goals

Forensic Scientists at Work

Forensic scientists may be asked to testify as experts in court. They must be prepared to answer questions from attorneys about their expertise and abilities.

Be sure to include in your presentation a caption that explains the context in which the image is used.

Because Brandon attends college in his home state, his tuition fees are lower than those of out-of-state students.

ACTIVITY

▶ Scoring Guide

Your instructor will use the rubric to the right to grade your presentation. High-scoring presentations will include multiple slides and will be delivered in a confident, professional manner.

Score	Guidelines for Multimedia Presentation
Excellent	Includes graphic element and images; data from reliable, credited sources; complete explanation of goal and steps to achieve goal; confident and smooth presentation style.
Good	Includes graphic element and one image; data from reliable, credited sources; good explanation of goal and steps to achieve goal; confident and smooth presentation style.
Fair	Lacks graphic elements, but includes one image; data from questionable, uncredited sources; brief explanation of goal and steps to achieve goal; awkward presentation style.
Poor	Lacks graphic elements and images; unreliable, uncredited sources; weak explanation of goal and steps to achieve goal; poor presentation style.

Selling Yourself, Again

GOALS

LEARN how to promote your achievements in the workplace . . . .
. 104–106

WRITE notes to model good workplace communication . . . .
. 106

PREPARE to think like a supervisor 107

TERMS

self-promotion

When you're seeking a job, you "sell" your skills and abilities to employers. Once you land a job, you should continue to use self-promotion in the workplace. **Self-promotion** means telling others about your positive traits and achievements.

Promoting your workplace achievements fulfills several goals. It helps bring your accomplishments to the attention of your superiors. It also lets you present yourself to co-workers as an honest, hard-working, and skilled employee.

Although self-promotion can prove beneficial, you should beware of its pitfalls. Self-promotion should be handled delicately. You don't want to come off as insincere or dishonest during this process. Don't kiss up to your boss or take credit for the work of others. Empty or flattering statements can make your supervisor less likely to promote you or take you seriously. You may come across as shallow and focused only on yourself and not the company.

The best kind of self-promotion is based in fact. You should point to measurable goals that you have achieved. These could be sales goals or less concrete achievements such as improving your written communication skills. Keep a record of these achievements as part of your promotion plan. Ask for a copy of any performance-related documentation, such as performance reviews or customer surveys.

ACTIVITY

▶ Self-Promotion

The employees below are promoting their achievements. Circle those statements that show good examples of self-promotion. Draw an "X" over those statements that show poor examples of self-promotion.

ACTIVITY

▶ **Hey, Look at Me!**

Think back to the group dynamics activity you completed in Chapter 2. Did you identify yourself as a leader or a follower? This could affect the way you promote your achievements to your supervisor at work. Revisit your responses from Chapter 2. Then make a personal plan to let your supervisor know of your successes. Use the questions below to guide your planning process.

1. Did you identify yourself as more of a leader or follower in Chapter 2? _____

2. How would you rather tell your supervisor about your accomplishments—by speaking face-to-face or through a note or e-mail? Explain your choice.

_____
_____
_____
_____

3. Based on your personality and comfort level, what behaviors should you increase to successfully promote yourself? What behaviors should you do less?

_____
_____
_____

"You look great today, Felicia! Is that a new haircut?"

"Hey, I got a perfect score on my secret shop!"

Strategies for Shy People

If you consider yourself shy, you are not alone. About 40 percent of Americans classify themselves as shy. At times, usually outgoing people may act shy when they are less confident. It's natural to feel shy when facing a challenge, such as a new job. But there are strategies you can use to overcome your shyness and achieve your career goals.

One of the first steps to overcoming shyness is to remain self-aware. Take notice of situations in which you behave shyly. When you recognize a situation like this, make a choice to speak up. It may seem difficult at first. But with time, it will get easier. By staying strong and focusing on your goal, you can overcome your shyness one day at a time.

Developing self-confidence represents another important step toward defeating shyness. There are many ways to build self-confidence.

- Give yourself extra time to prepare an important task or assignment.

- Think more positively about situations in which you must interact with co-workers. Visualize a company meeting as a supportive—rather than as a threatening—environment. This may help you feel more at ease in speaking up at such meetings.

- Finally, take small steps to move out of your comfort zone. You can't change your personality from shy to outgoing overnight. But by building good communication habits, you will gradually begin to feel and act less shy.

Your input is valuable. Take advantage of opportunities to make your ideas known.

ACTIVITY

▶ ### Just a Note

Employees in many different jobs communicate in writing. For example, a nursing home attendant may write a note about patient care. In many jobs, you might write notes telling other employees what tasks have been completed.

Writing notes can also be a good communication technique for shy employees. These workers can write notes to inform supervisors of their accomplishments. Study the two examples shown below. Then on the final sticky note, write to your instructor describing your accomplishments over the past week.

I completed the virus check on your computer and installed QuickBooks Pro 2011.

Mrs. West ate very little dinner last night. She had a cold and went to sleep around 8:30 p.m.

IN FOCUS: EMPLOYABILITY AND CAREER DEVELOPMENT

Thinking Like a Supervisor

Thinking like a supervisor can help you in several ways. First, you can begin to understand your supervisor's responsibilities. This might help you to be better prepared if you receive the promotion you hope for. But more importantly, thinking like a supervisor can help you to improve in your current job. Such improvement will help strengthen your case for a future promotion.

As a supervisor, what types of traits would you look for in your employees? You might suggest traits such as punctuality, honesty, and dedication. You would want employees who strive to meet their goals. When you identify key traits, it will also be important for you to display these traits in your own work. Modeling such behavior may lead to a promotion.

Bill (right) enjoys going to lunch with Chris and Jenifer (left, seated), but he always remembers to be professional.

Managing Former Co-Workers

Getting a promotion is a cause for celebration! However, a promotion can have some potential drawbacks. One example occurs when promoted employees find themselves managing former co-workers. This type of situation can prove awkward for those involved. The best way to handle such a case is to remain professional, whether you are an entry-level employee or a supervisor.

You may enjoy socializing and sharing personal stories with your co-workers. But what if you're promoted? Your former co-workers may become your direct reports. What if they know that you have made poor decisions or taken part in risky behaviors? That might cause them to lose respect for you as a boss. Without respect, it is very difficult for a supervisor to lead.

Because Bill (standing) has always behaved in a professional manner, Chris and Jenifer respect him now that he has been promoted to senior sales manager.

Mentoring and Managing

TERMS

delegate

motivation

In Chapter 1, you learned that a mentor can help you to find your way when learning a new job. Remember that a mentor is a more experienced employee who offers guidance to a new employee. As you gain experience in a job, you may get the chance to become a mentor to a new employee.

To learn how to become a mentor, look no further than the people who acted as mentors to you. Think about what you learned from them. What would you like to pass on to a newer employee? In addition to helping new workers find their way around, good mentors might also teach job-related skills. They can share information about employers. At times, mentors can help employees with difficult challenges. They can also offer tips for improving job performance. The checklist to the right identifies key qualities that a successful mentor should possess.

Good Mentor Checklist

- ☑ Displays a willingness to devote time to mentoring a new employee
- ☑ Shows both honesty and integrity
- ☑ Possesses strong communication skills
- ☑ Holds a track record of success in the workplace
- ☑ Works effectively with individuals from many diverse backgrounds
- ☑ Demonstrates sensitivity to the feelings of the employees being mentored

It is essential that a mentor behaves professionally. Mentors are very important as trainers and support staff. People often remember more qualities about their mentor than they do about their supervisors.

ACTIVITY

▶ **Identify Your Mentors**

Think about people who have mentored or influenced you. They may be from your personal life or from previous jobs. List below what you have learned from your mentors. Then think about ways in which you might have acted as a mentor to others.

_____

_____

_____

Becoming a Mentor

The first step in becoming a good mentor is having a positive attitude. An upbeat attitude can help the employees you mentor develop a positive outlook at work.

A good mentor should also have advanced workplace skills. Ideally, mentors seek to pass along both a positive attitude and workplace knowledge and skills. This explains why mentors tend to be both very experienced and highly skilled.

> ▶ **PLAY** VIDEO ❯
>
> ***Be The Mentor*** Jamal has worked very hard since his first day on the job back in Chapter 1 and now serves as a mentor to other employees. Watch how Jamal uses his experience to mentor his co-worker Nicki when she needs advice.
>
>
> **DVD**
> Video 8
>
> **Watch the video. Then answer the questions below.**
>
> **1.** Why did Nicki approach Jamal with her problem?
>
> _____
>
> **2.** How did Jamal act as a positive mentor to Nicki?
>
> _____
>
> **3.** How did Nicki handle her meeting with Javier?
>
> _____
>
> **4.** How did Nicki benefit from having Jamal as a mentor?
>
> _____

COMMUNICATION

Active Listening

Think back to what you learned about active listening skills in Chapter 2. You can use these same skills when mentoring a fellow employee. These skills will prove especially useful when listening to and responding to an employee's workplace challenges or problems.

Use the following tips to become a better active listener:

1. Listen attentively when a co-worker discusses a workplace problem with you. Resist the urge to interrupt until the person finishes speaking.

2. Maintain eye contact as you listen. This will show your co-worker that he or she has your undivided attention.

3. Pay attention to your co-worker's body language as you listen. What do the person's posture and gestures tell you about his or her emotions?

4. Demonstrate that you hear—and understand— what your co-worker is saying. For example, nod your head as the person speaks. This will silently communicate your focus on the person's words. When the speaker has finished, paraphrase aloud his or her concerns. For example, if told by Jim that a fellow co-worker disregarded his input, you'd say, "So Jim, it sounds like you believe that Linda doesn't respect your opinion."

Management

Managers and mentors can also be very different. For example, managers have additional responsibilities beyond the duties of a mentor. Managers often must delegate tasks to direct reports. To **delegate** means to give another the power to act for you. Delegating allows employees the chance to grow. It also allows a manager to see how well their employees are performing.

Managers need solid communication skills. They must often relay information to many people in the company. Good communication can help increase employee performance. It also cuts down on confusion. Strong managers should also be well organized. For example, supervisors need to know how best to complete workplace tasks. They must schedule the correct amount of employees. At times, they will need to delegate assignments. When making such decisions, managers always should consider the bigger picture.

Any good manager makes sure that his or her employees are educated about their jobs. Knowledgeable employees are confident and perform their jobs well.

ACTIVITY

▶ ## Be the Manager

Suppose that, for the next week, you will manage this class. Ask your instructor to provide you with a list of concepts, information, or tasks that will be covered during this time.

Using this information, develop a plan to organize class activities. Make sure that your plan covers all the requirements. These are the types of decisions that managers make every day. They often have to make them on their own, without input from other employees.

_____

_____

_____

_____

_____

_____

IN FOCUS: EMPLOYABILITY AND CAREER DEVELOPMENT

Management Responsibilities

The illustrations on this page show the role of a restaurant's manager in relation to the restaurant's structure. Andrew, the manager, has responsibilities to the restaurant's owner, employees, and customers.

As the manager, he needs to incorporate feedback from customers and his staff to improve the restaurant. Andrew is ultimately responsible to the restaurant owner, so he must communicate honestly with her about staff and finances.

OWNER
The restaurant's owner expects Andrew to run a profitable business. She provides him with sales goals. Andrew informs her when he needs to spend additional money on staff or equipment.

CUSTOMER
Customer feedback is very important to any successful restaurant. Andrew takes all comments seriously and acts to correct problems.

BACK OF HOUSE (BOH)
Back-of-house staff (chef, cooks, dishwashers) work in restaurant kitchens. They inform Andrew about the length of time it takes them to prepare orders and the supplies they need. He guides them to prepare food and use equipment safely.

FRONT OF HOUSE (FOH)
The front-of-house staff includes hosts, servers, and bussers. They interact with customers and give Andrew feedback. He instructs his FOH staff on how to deliver excellent service.

RESTAURANT MANAGER, ANDREW
As a restaurant manager, Andrew answers to his boss, the owner. He's also responsible for managing all employees. Andrew also listens closely to the customers. An effective manager balances the direction he or she receives from the owner with feedback he or she receives from other employees and customers.

 To learn more about communication strategies, see Appendix C.

Management Challenges

Managers must be prepared to face the challenges that come with extra responsibilities. For instance, some companies may give managers specific performance goals that they are expected to achieve. Managers must determine how best to use available resources to meet or surpass these goals.

One important management challenge is working with difficult employees.

Another management challenge involves working with employees of different ability levels. If an employee fails to meet your expectations, you should help him or her improve. You may try motivation, additional training, or even disciplinary action. **Motivation** means providing a person with a reason for doing something. When employees do well, you should recognize and reward their performance.

LEADERSHIP AND TEAMWORK

Budget Your Workforce

As a manager, you may be required to plan a weekly budget. To do this, you need to answer several questions. First, you need to determine the amount of hours you have to fill. Then, you have to figure out which employees to schedule to cover this time. You must also know each employee's pay rate, as well as the number of hours he or she can work.

For this activity, assume that a full-time employee works between 35 and 40 hours per week. It's important that these employees work at least 35 hours. They must do this to maintain their full-time status. A part-time employee can work between 10 and 20 hours per week.

Now, suppose you are the manager. Choose a sample scenario from those presented on pages 138–139. The scenarios provide the following information:

- the amount of hours you have to schedule
- the workplace's total weekly budget for wages
- the positions you need to schedule
- the employees who work in each job
- the number of hours each employee can work
- the pay rate for each employee

Using this information, create a weekly budget for your workforce.

Your budget should include the following information:

- the days and times that employees are scheduled to work
- the total number of hours each employee works
- the total weekly pay that each employee receives
- your weekly labor costs (total weekly pay of all employees)

Use the sample schedule and callouts (page 113) as a model for your schedule and budget. When you have completed your budget, compare it with a classmate who used the same scenario.

Hands-Off Management

Workplace demands often make it difficult for managers to watch every employee. Because close monitoring may be hard in certain businesses, some managers take a more hands-off approach. This doesn't mean that they give up control, or that they're no longer important. Instead, these managers trust their employees to handle certain tasks. This allows managers time to focus on specialized work that only they can complete.

As a hands-off manager, you may delegate more work to your employees. However, you would also have to train employees properly for additional tasks. You should create a system to regularly check their work and ensure its quality.

The manager of a day-care provider might find a hands-off management style to be more effective when supervising numerous teachers across several different classrooms.

This figure shows the budget for a full week of wages. The total weekly cost must be less than the budget.

This schedule shows which shifts that each employee works. It also shows wages paid each day.

Use the space below to create your schedule.

WEEKLY BUDGET:
$1,000
Employees & Wages

Ahmed: $20/hr/FT
Evelyn: $15/hr/PT
Leon: $10/hr/PT

This list identifies employees who are available to work. It also gives their status and hourly wages.

Hanover Park
PARK RANGERS WEEKLY SCHEDULE

	9AM-1PM	2PM-6PM	Daily Wages
Monday	Leon	Evelyn	$100
Tuesday	Evelyn	Evelyn	$120
Wednesday	Ahmed	Ahmed	$160
Thursday	Ahmed	Ahmed	$160
Friday	Ahmed	Ahmed	$160
Saturday	Ahmed	Ahmed	$160
Sunday	Leon	Ahmed	$120
		Total Weekly Cost	$980

This figure gives the total amount that was spent on employee wages during the week.

Chapter Recap

Using the list below, place a check mark next to the goals you achieved in Chapter 4.

▶ **In Lesson 1, you . . .**

❒ Learned about working effectively in a diverse workplace

❒ Studied examples of workplace discrimination and harassment

❒ Interpreted discrimination and harassment policies

▶ **In Lesson 2, you . . .**

❒ Completed a list of short- and long-term goals

❒ Examined strategies for earning a raise or promotion

❒ Prepared to leave one job and accept another

▶ **In Lesson 3, you . . .**

❒ Learned the types of training, certification, and degrees you need to reach your career goals

❒ Studied the ways employers help employees learn new skills

❒ Applied what you learned to update your resume

▶ **In Lesson 4, you . . .**

❒ Learned how to promote your achievements in the workplace

❒ Wrote notes to model good workplace communication

❒ Prepared to think like a supervisor

▶ **In Lesson 5, you . . .**

❒ Learned how to mentor other employees in the workplace

❒ Examined the additional responsibilities that come with being a manager

❒ Applied management skills

Chapter Review

Name: _____ Date: _____

▶ **Directions:** Choose the best answer.

1. Which of the following is an example of cultural sensitivity?

   A. asking your co-workers personal questions
   B. complimenting a co-worker on his or her appearance
   C. forwarding humorous e-mails to your co-workers
   D. respecting the religious beliefs of your co-workers

▶ **Directions:** Determine whether the following statements are true or false. If the statement is true, write T. If the statement is false, write F. Then rewrite the false statement to make it true.

2. Most forms of workplace discrimination are easy to spot.

   _____

   _____

3. Once people have been hired for a job, they should put their resumes aside until they are ready to look for jobs again.

   _____

   _____

▶ **Directions:** Write your answer to the questions below.

4. How are discrimination and harassment alike? How are they different?

   _____

   _____

   _____

▶ **Directions:** Match the terms in the left column to the correct definition in the right column.

_____ 5. corporate structure

_____ 6. promoted

_____ 7. notice

_____ 8. self-promotion

_____ 9. delegate

A. telling others about your achievements
B. advanced to a higher-ranking position
C. the organization of a company's employees and departments
D. an announcement that an employee is leaving
E. to give another the power to act for you

Chapter Review

Adapting to Changing Responsibilities

▶ Think about a time in your life when you had to take on extra responsibilities. This might include having a child or caring for a family member. You could also consider times when you added new activities to your daily life, such as going to college or getting a job.

10. Describe this experience in the space below.

_____

_____

_____

_____

_____

_____

_____

11. Think back to the experience you described above. In the space below, explain how you successfully balanced your new responsibilities with your existing duties. Identify effective techniques and discuss any actions that you would do differently.

_____

_____

_____

_____

_____

_____

_____

12. When you get a promotion at work, it's similar to tackling new responsibilities in life. Review the strategies you've identified above. Then highlight or underline those that will also be useful in managing new responsibilities at work.

Name: _____   Date: _____

Mentoring

▶ When did you last learn a new concept or skill? It may have been when you started a new job or when you chose to volunteer with a local organization. You also may have learned new skills for parenting or serving as a leader of a team or a group.

13. As you reflect, recall the information you learned in the space below. List the advice you were given. Then identify information that you wish someone had shared with you about that particular situation.

_____

_____

_____

_____

_____

_____

_____

_____

_____

_____

_____

14. Suppose that you will serve as a mentor to someone in a similar position. In the space below, list the information that you would share with this person.

Mentoring Checklist

☐ _____

_____

_____

☐ _____

_____

_____

☐ _____

_____

_____

☐ _____

_____

_____

☐ _____

_____

_____

☐ _____

_____

_____

Allocating Time

▶ Effective managers must learn how to successfully allocate, or divide and distribute, time. This involves analyzing the amount of work to be done and the correct number of staff needed to complete it in a certain amount of time. Imagine you are the manager in the activities below. Allocate time and plan staffing for two different businesses using the information provided.

15. Suppose you are the manager of a coffee shop. Each morning, the shop experiences a rush between 7 AM and 9 AM. You currently have three employees scheduled to work during that time each morning. Each employee can serve one customer every four minutes.

What volume of customers would you need in order to schedule a fourth employee to serve all of them during the morning rush hours?

_____

_____

16. Suppose you are the manager of a quick oil-change shop. You need to schedule employees to work on Saturday, when the shop is open from 8 AM to 1 PM. You schedule employees based on the number of appointments you anticipate each Saturday.

This Saturday you expect 60 appointments. Each oil change lasts 15 minutes. How many employees will you need to schedule this day?

_____

_____

_____

Conflict Resolution

Recall the following steps to resolve conflicts:

1. Determine the cause of the conflict.
2. Ask the employees involved to clearly express their sides of the dispute.
3. Encourage the employees to consider one another's view.
4. Invite the employees to describe their ideal resolution of the conflict.
5. Choose the solution that works best for everyone, especially the business.

Researchers have determined several reasons why workplace conflict occurs. Each type of conflict fits into one of the following eight categories:

CAUSES OF CONFLICT

Cause	Description
Different needs	This type of conflict occurs when people share resources such as space, equipment, money, or a supervisor's time. For example, conflict may occur if two employees share a computer.
Different styles	People have different styles when working or leading. At times, a co-worker or supervisor may have a different style than you. For example, your supervisor may be lax in enforcing rules, but you believe they should be strictly enforced.
Different perceptions	People may interpret one situation in different ways. You may believe that a co-worker understood that when he finished one task he should move on to another. But he may think that you were going to give him further instructions. This difference in perception may lead to conflict.
Different goals	Co-workers often have different goals. Some people may want to be promoted quickly. Others just want to perform well in their current positions. A more assertive employee may conflict with a more passive one.
Different pressures	The tasks a worker performs may affect the way that he or she feels pressure. For example, a cook in a fast-food restaurant may feel less pressure than the cashier who serves impatient customers.
Different roles	Sometimes an employer will ask an employee to take on another role or task. As a result, co-workers who regularly fill that role may believe the supervisor doesn't think they are doing a good job. As a result, the employees may act negatively toward the helpers.
Different personal values	Co-workers may have different personal values. Perhaps you believe that everyone should arrive 15 minutes early. A co-worker may believe in simply arriving on time. This difference of opinion may lead to conflict.
Uncertainty	People like to know the rules. If a company or supervisor is unclear about expectations, people may become nervous and uncertain. Two co-workers could easily have different interpretations of a policy or procedure. This may lead to conflict.

People also react to conflict in many different ways. To find the best resolution, you must understand the way parties may react.

- **The competitor:** Some people react to conflict in a competitive way. They stand firmly behind their ideas and can persuade others to conform to their point of view. It can be difficult to change their opinions.

- **The collaborator:** Collaborative people like to find a solution that works for everyone. They ask all parties for suggestions. At times, they may take a long time to arrive at a solution.

- **The compromiser:** Most people will compromise when faced with a conflict. However, compromisers should be careful not to give up too much. This could lead to resentment and further conflict.

- **The accommodator:** Some people are uncomfortable with conflict. They will do whatever they can to resolve it, even though it may not be in their best interest. While it's good to be accommodating, people should avoid taking it too far.

- **The avoider:** An avoider will ignore conflict rather than deal with it. He or she will not participate in the resolution. Avoiders may believe that their needs are unimportant.

Now that you know and understand the causes, reactions, and the steps to resolve conflict, you are in a better position to effectively manage conflict in the workplace.

Training, Certification, and Degrees

Employees can take steps to better themselves in any job. These steps may help them improve their job performance, learn new job-related skills, and prepare for a better job in the future. Additional training, certification, or education can be an important step to improving your career. If you decide to pursue these opportunities, you will discover many available options. You should weigh these options carefully so that you make the best choice for you and your career.

In the space at the bottom of the page, list local resources from which you could obtain additional training, a new certification, or a degree. You may identify resources such as community colleges or for-profit universities. Many local communities also offer training programs for residents, particularly in computer- and technology-related fields. For each resource you list, write a brief description of how the degree or certification it offers might help you improve your job performance or advance in your chosen career. You may gather information about these resources in several ways:

- Try talking with friends, family members, or co-workers. They can share their experiences and give advice.

- Ask people who work in your field for their opinions. They may offer insight into which resources provide the best possible benefit to you and your career.

- Consult Internet resources, job centers, or a government benefits office. Check to see whether financial support is available.

_____

_____

_____

_____

_____

_____

_____

Advantages of Continuing Education

It's a good practice to explore educational opportunities—especially when you have a job. By building on your existing skills, you become more valuable to your employer. You'll also make yourself more marketable to other employers. This is important should you lose your job or decide to seek a better position elsewhere.

Think carefully about your continuing education options. Take an honest look at your current job performance. Identify areas in which you could benefit from additional knowledge or skills. Taking these steps will allow you to expand your qualifications or improve any weak skills.

The graph below demonstrates the benefits of continuing education. Workers with more education earn more money. Simply put, people with bachelor's degrees earn $1 million more over their lifetime than people without high school diplomas.

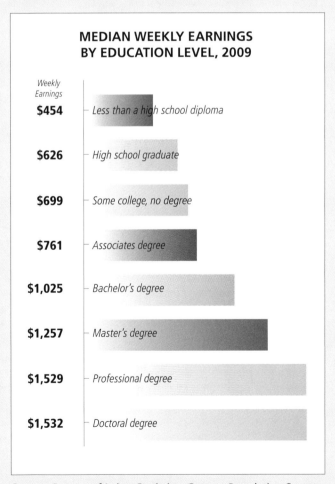

MEDIAN WEEKLY EARNINGS BY EDUCATION LEVEL, 2009

Weekly Earnings	
$454	Less than a high school diploma
$626	High school graduate
$699	Some college, no degree
$761	Associates degree
$1,025	Bachelor's degree
$1,257	Master's degree
$1,529	Professional degree
$1,532	Doctoral degree

Source: Bureau of Labor Statistics, Current Population Survey

Paying for Additional Training

Determining how to pay for additional training can be almost as important as choosing the right type of training. The first step involves determining whether you qualify for government aid. A variety of federal student loan programs are available to students in the United States. They offer more favorable terms than other financing choices. For example, federal student loans typically have lower interest rates and less restrictive credit requirements than private loans.

When using loans to finance additional learning, it's important to understand the difference between subsidized and unsubsidized loans. A **subsidized loan** is granted based on a student's financial need. Students with subsidized loans are not charged interest until they begin repaying the loan after leaving school. Until that time, this interest is paid, or subsidized, by the federal government.

An **unsubsidized loan** requires that you begin paying interest immediately. The interest on unsubsidized loans is also capitalized. This means that you pay *additional* interest on the interest that accumulates on your loan. Over time, the extra interest paid on an unsubsidized loan can make it much more expensive than a subsidized loan.

Legally, you can use loan money to pay for any costs associated with a training, certification, or degree program. This includes tuition, as well as books, housing, and other related expenses. However, remember that these loans *must* be repaid. Unlike other debts, student loans must be repaid even if you file for bankruptcy.

Research your options when taking on an educational loan. It's crucial to know and understand the loan terms. If you don't understand the terms in these documents, ask the lending officer for an explanation.

Think carefully about the amount of money you will truly need for your education. Consider Raymon, who attended a for-profit university in order to become a certified LPN. He could have worked a part-time job and borrowed less money. But the university encouraged him to accept all of the loans he was offered. Raymon had a huge amount of debt when he graduated. Even with a higher salary, he cannot afford his loan payments.

Examples like Raymon's demonstrate the importance of thinking critically about your decisions regarding loans. In many cases, you may find it best to only take on loans that cover the cost of your tuition and books. You may have to work part-time in order to cover your other expenses. But you'll be burdened with far less debt when you finish your training. This will allow you to pay off your debts more quickly. You will also have greater flexibility to choose a job based on factors beyond the one that pays the best.

Many of the costs of additional education are offset by their long-term benefits. As the bar graph below shows, people with more education are less likely to be unemployed. Those with degrees also earn higher starting salaries. Earning additional money means that you should have the necessary income to pay off any education loans.

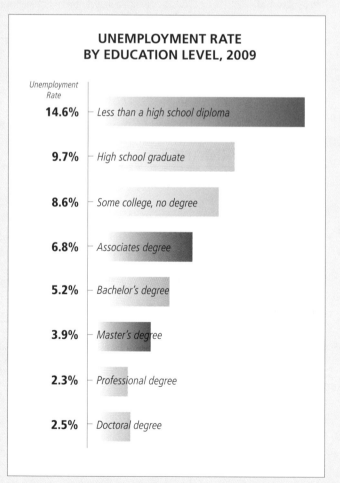

UNEMPLOYMENT RATE BY EDUCATION LEVEL, 2009

Unemployment Rate

14.6%	Less than a high school diploma
9.7%	High school graduate
8.6%	Some college, no degree
6.8%	Associates degree
5.2%	Bachelor's degree
3.9%	Master's degree
2.3%	Professional degree
2.5%	Doctoral degree

Source: Bureau of Labor Statistics, Current Population Survey

APPENDIX C

Communication Strategies

You have learned that strong communication skills are vital to becoming an effective employee. These skills affect your ability to succeed in your career. Important communication skills include working with a supervisor and providing good customer service. Use the information below to review the communication strategies provided throughout the chapters of *Effective Employee*.

STARTING OFF

Situation	Strategies
Communicating with your supervisor	Adapt your style of communication to match that of your supervisor. Look for verbal and nonverbal clues to learn how he or she interacts with employees. Model your communication on his or her style for interactions such as calling in sick, reporting that you will be late to work, and requesting time off from work.
Working with different communication styles	Your co-workers likely will use a variety of different communication styles. At times, you may have to make polite requests of these individuals in order to communicate effectively. For instance, you might have to ask a "fast talker" to repeat what he or she says. By remaining polite and respectful, you will aid communication and avoid conflict in the workplace.
Learning the lingo of your industry	Ask your co-workers to explain industry lingo, or unfamiliar terms that specifically relate to your field. Commit these terms to memory and practice using them in the course of your work. Mentors can be particularly helpful in clarifying the meanings of industry lingo.

WORKPLACE SKILLS

Situation	Strategies
Professional communication in customer service	Always behave in a professional manner around customers. Remain calm and treat customers with respect, even if they become upset with you.
	Speak clearly when assisting a customer. When they have a problem, customers want someone who can help them quickly and professionally.
	Practice active listening when interacting with customers. Listening carefully and responding thoughtfully shows that you understand customers' problems. Active listening techniques will also help you plan a solution to these problems.
	Paraphrase customer feedback to help clarify their views. This will help you solve problems more effectively.

JOB PERFORMANCE

Situation	Strategies
Listening through stress to understand feedback	Stress can make it hard to listen carefully to your supervisor's feedback. To help stay focused, maintain eye contact with your supervisor. Repeat his or her words in your head. You should take written notes to remember feedback.
Gathering missing information	Your employer often makes decisions based in part on information that you may lack. As a result, you may face instructions or expectations that seem unfair. Rather than become upset, try to gather missing information from your supervisor. This can allow you to see the bigger picture.

SUCCESS ON THE JOB

Situation	Strategies
Squashing inappropriate workplace communication	If a co-worker brings up an inappropriate topic in the workplace, try to quickly change the subject. This will send a clear signal to the co-worker that the topic does not belong in the workplace.
Active listening as a mentor	As a mentor, you should listen and respond to employees' workplace problems. By practicing active listening, you can gain a better understanding of these problems and be better prepared to solve them. Avoid interrupting, maintain eye contact, observe employees' body language, and paraphrase employees' concerns back to them. These steps will show that you understand employee concerns.

Table Manners and Restaurant Etiquette

As a holiday gift, Dr. Mauro decided to take her staff to a nice dinner. She chose an expensive Italian restaurant as the destination. One of her receptionists, Marta, felt nervous about attending this event. She was worried that she would not understand the menu or know which fork to use at the proper time during the meal. Rather than be embarrassed in front of her boss and co-workers, Marta considered skipping the dinner. Perhaps you have found yourself in a similar situation. However, like Marta, you needn't worry about situations like this one. By following the basic rules on this page, you can order and dine confidently at almost any restaurant.

The tips to the right will help you to practice proper restaurant etiquette when dining with co-workers. These simple steps will allow you to relax and enjoy these gatherings, without worrying that you unwittingly will do something inappropriate or embarrassing. Following these instructions will also allow you to make a positive impression on your co-workers and—most importantly—your boss.

The diagram below shows a place setting similar to what you might find at a business lunch or dinner. Examine the various components in this place setting. Then you can comfortably use each item for its intended purpose.

- Place your napkin in your lap as soon as you are seated at the table. If you leave the table during the meal, loosely fold the napkin and place it to the side of your plate.

- Ask your servers about unfamiliar terms or dishes on the menu. Explaining these items is part of their job.

- If you cannot pronounce the name of a menu item, it's okay to point to it. You can also ask the server for a recommendation. They may pronounce and explain unfamiliar menu items.

- Always taste your food before adding salt, pepper, or other seasonings. Be sure to chew with your mouth closed, and avoid talking with your mouth full.

- For hard-to-scoop items, use a knife or piece of bread to move them onto your fork. Don't pick up or push around food with your fingers.

- When you've finished eating, don't stack your dishes. Your server will gather them when he or she clears the table.

- Take cues from your boss. If he or she decides to order dessert or an alcoholic beverage, it's okay for you to do the same. But remember, you want to use these gatherings to impress, not to become an office joke.

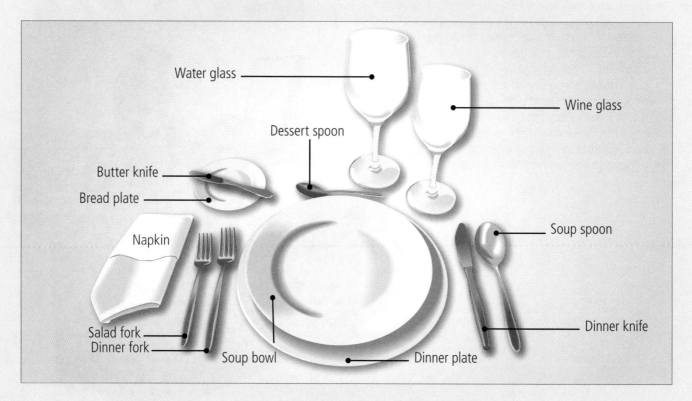

Water glass — Wine glass — Dessert spoon — Butter knife — Bread plate — Napkin — Soup spoon — Salad fork — Dinner fork — Soup bowl — Dinner plate — Dinner knife

Workplace Technology

In Chapter 2, you learned about problems that can arise in the workplace from inappropriate postings on social networking sites, such as Facebook or Twitter. The use of these sites is only one of many potential obstacles that workers face in today's technology-driven workplaces.

Employers today often supply the phones and computers needed to perform job-related tasks. Companies can and do monitor how employees use these devices. Improper use of these items can lead to disciplinary action and even termination. These strategies will help you to comply with company policies regarding the use of company-owned technology.

- Avoid making personal phone calls during working hours—especially on company phones. Companies can easily monitor your phone usage and verify whether you are using the phone for company business.

- Avoid visiting Web sites unrelated to your work on company time. Much like phone records, companies have the ability to monitor your Internet usage. Your employer may see that you often visit your favorite Web sites. Employers value productive employees. Don't get caught visiting eBay or Facebook when you should be working.

- Limit personal use of company e-mail accounts. Companies can monitor your company e-mail account. These e-mails are considered the property of the company. The company can examine them whenever it wants. Therefore, you should never send a company e-mail with negative comments about a co-worker or supervisor. Also, avoid sending inappropriate or offensive e-mails from your work account. This holds true whether you are e-mailing people inside or outside of the company.

Some companies require employees to sign **confidentiality agreements**. These documents state that employees cannot share information about the company's business that could prove valuable to competitors. Confidentiality agreements usually cover all forms of communication, such as a simple conversation, a text message, or even a video chat.

For example, Joanna works for a software company. Suppose that she sends an e-mail to a friend saying she was developing a new software program. This likely violates Joanna's confidentiality agreement even if she mentioned it casually. Companies take these agreements very seriously. A single violation could lead to termination. As a result, you should always be cautious when communicating and avoid breaching the trust that your employer places in you.

Additional Resources

▶ **GLOSSARY**

▶ **INDEX**

▶ **ANSWER KEY**

▶ **SAMPLE MANAGEMENT SCENARIOS**

▶ **VIDEO INSTRUCTIONS**

Glossary

A

active listening: listening carefully and responding thoughtfully to another person to show that you understand their views or issues

C

chain of command: the structure of authority in an organization

compensation: payment for services

compromise: a settlement of a dispute in which each party gives up some of its demands

confidentiality agreements: documents, usually signed by both employee and employer, that state that employees cannot share information about the company's business that could prove valuable to competitors

conflict: a strong disagreement between two people

constructive feedback: comments meant to address workplace performance issues and encourage improvement and growth

co-pay: an out-of-pocket payment you must make each time you seek medical care

corporate culture: the set of often unwritten values and practices that workers follow

corporate structure: the way in which a company's jobs and departments are organized

cost-of-living increases: small raises in salary designed to offset increasing prices of housing and consumer goods from one year to the next

CPR/AED: cardiopulmonary resuscitation (CPR) and automated external defibrillator (AED); life-saving procedures designed to add air to the lungs and compress the chest of a victim—the AED delivers an electronic shock to jump-start a victim's heart

cultural sensitivity: an awareness of differences between cultures

customer: any person or organization that buys or receives a good or service

D

deductibles: the amounts you must pay before insurance begins to cover your expenses

delegate: to give another the power to act for you

dependent: a person who relies on another for financial support

direct reports: the employees who work directly for a given supervisor

disciplinary action: measures used to correct employee behavior

discrimination: unfair treatment of a person or group of people based on certain characteristics, such as race or religion

diverse: made up of many different parts or characteristics

G

gender: a person's sex, either male or female

grievances: complaints or problems

gross wages: the amount you earned before any deductions or taxes are subtracted

group dynamic: all of the different roles and interactions that make up a group

H

harassment: behavior intended to disturb or upset another employee

hygiene: the ways a person stays clean and healthy

I

infer: to draw a reasonable conclusion based on available information

L

lingo: the vocabulary that relates specifically to a particular field

LLC: a limited liability company; common for a small business to protect the owner's property and other assets

M

mentor: a more experienced employee who offers guidance to a new employee

merit increase: a raise in salary an employee earns because of outstanding performance

motivation: providing a person with a reason for doing something

N

net wages: the amount of money you receive after deducting taxes and benefits

networking: the process of building relationships with other people that will benefit your career

notice: a warning or announcement; in the workplace, this is an announcement that a worker plans to leave the organization

O

objective: dealing with facts without letting one's feelings interfere with them

OSHA: the Occupational Safety and Health Administration; a government agency that regulates workplace safety

P

paraphrase: to restate something in your own words

pay grade: a certain level of payment that an employee can reach for the work they perform

policies: workplace rules and regulations

procedure: step-by-step instructions for completing important tasks

professional: behaving in a polite, respectful, and businesslike style

promoted: when a worker is advanced to a higher-ranking position

R

reimbursement: being paid back by your company for work-related expenses

S

self-discipline: having the willpower to do the tasks expected of you

self-esteem: a feeling of confidence and satisfaction with oneself

self-promotion: telling others about your positive traits and achievements

sensitive: a condition in which the attitudes and feelings of others affect you

shift: the time during which you are at work

stress: a condition that produces physical or mental tension

stressors: events that cause stress

subsidized loan: a loan granted based on a student's financial need; interest on this type of loan is paid (subsidized) by the federal government until the student leaves school and begins repayment

support staff: workers, such as receptionists, secretaries, assistants, and information technologists, who support the work of other staff members

U

unsubsidized loan: a loan granted based on financial need, usually offered in addition to subsidized loans; interest accumulates on this type of loan immediately—it is not paid by the federal government

W

wage reductions: items such as retirement contributions or health insurance

wages: payment or money received for working

Index

Note: Page numbers in **bold** indicate definitions.

NOTES

Answer Key

CHAPTER 1

PAGE 2
VIDEO 1: *First Day On The Job*
1. Jamal's supervisor and fellow employees make him feel welcome by introducing themselves, being polite, and answering all of his questions.
2. Javier showed Jamal around the restaurant and pointed out where and when the weekly schedule is posted. He also told Jamal that Tina would mentor him. Tina will show him how to clock in, take orders, work the POS system for entering orders, and deal with customers.
3. Jamal needed these documents to fill out his new-hire paperwork.

PAGE 4
ACADEMIC FOUNDATIONS: MATHEMATICS— *Taxes and Your Paycheck*
1. 1200 – 155 = 1045
   152.08 x 2 = 304.16
   1045 – 304.16 = 740.84
   740.84 – 434 = 306.84 x .15 = 46.03
   434 – 252 = 182 x .10 = 18.20
   46.03 + 18.20 = 64.23
   The amount of federal income tax that would be withheld from Heather's paycheck is $64.23.

PAGE 5
ACTIVITY: *Learn Your Way Around*

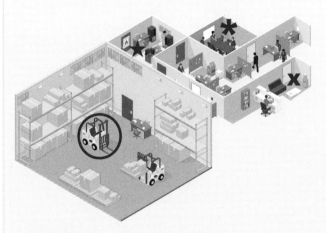

PAGE 6
ACTIVITY: *Decoding Workplace Schedules*
1. 8 hours
2. 21 hours
3. Denard
4. Reynaldo
5. 10 days
6. 4 days
7. 7 AM to 3 PM

PAGE 10
ACTIVITY: *Understanding Workplace Policies*
1. No, the company policy states that employees cannot possess weapons on company property.
2. Harassment is behavior that bothers or offends another employee and prevents that person from doing his or her job.
3. This employee would have accumulated four days of vacation pay by the end of the year.

PAGE 13
ACTIVITY: *Procedures for FMLA*
1. 2
2. 4
3. 5
4. 1
5. 6
6. 3

PAGE 15
ACTIVITY: *Health Plan A or B?*
Students' paragraphs should identify their choice of a health plan and cite the specifics of their chosen plan to support their decision.

PAGE 17
ACTIVITY: *Understand Training Manuals*
Students' responses will vary, but questions should relate to the structure and purpose of employee training manuals, and should be answerable using the content of the excerpt.

PAGE 18
ACTIVITY: *Safety Warnings*
Students should cite examples of warning signs that may be found in the workplace of their chosen professions.

PAGE 20
VIDEO 2: *Mentoring*
1. Tina showed Jamal how to take orders and enter them into the POS system correctly. She gave Jamal a tip about repeating orders back to the customer for accuracy. She also told Jamal that he should not use his cell phone or text while on the job.

2. Jamal actively listens to Tina when she gives him information. Jamal then asks for confirmation after he does something to make sure he is doing it correctly.
3. Tina makes one mistake. She blames Betty for forgetting to sign out of the POS system and says that Betty is always forgetting something. Jamal should not respond to this remark and wait to work with Betty to form his own opinion.
4. Jamal will provide great customer service and know how to use the ordering system correctly.

PAGES 22–25
PATHWAYS: *Technology in the Workplace*
Activity: Analyze GIS Data
1. Most of the mineral deposits are located near the center of the state.
2. A cement company may establish a factory in the southeast part of the state, near the limestone deposits.
3. The oil filtration company may be better off locating in South Carolina because there is a larger supply of Fuller's Earth than there is of Kaolin.
4. Students' conclusions may vary, but should include the amount and variety of natural resources in South Carolina that have commercial (business) uses.

PAGE 27
ACTIVITY: *Cultural Clues*
A. The company sponsors a softball team to boost company morale.
B. The company has season tickets to a local sports team. They give them to employees, allow employees to purchase them, or award them to employees as prizes.
C. Employees chip in to purchase birthday cakes for co-workers on their birthdays.
D. A group of co-workers attends happy hour at a local bar after work.
E. Employees are allowed to wear headphones and listen to music while they work.

PAGE 29
ACTIVITY: *Where Do You Fit In?*
1. Possible response: I would read those materials provided by the employer that directly explain parts of the corporate culture. I would also observe and ask questions of my co-workers to learn about the corporate culture.

2. Possible response: I would feel comfortable taking a turn to purchase donuts for my co-workers for a Donut Friday tradition in the workplace. This activity would be a good way to build camaraderie with my co-workers. There would also be little risk of upsetting or offending anyone through this activity.
3. Possible response: I would not feel comfortable participating in an after-hours happy hour. While it could be enjoyable to hang out with co-workers, I would prefer to avoid social aspects of corporate culture in which employees are consuming alcohol.

Chapter 1 Review

PAGES 31–34
1. B
2. F; With each dependent you claim on your W-4 form, the government withholds less money from your paycheck.
3. T
4. An employee can learn about the company's corporate culture by observing the behavior of other employees and by asking questions.
5. C
6. E
7. B
8. A
9. D

Review: Make a Fire Escape Plan
10. and 11.

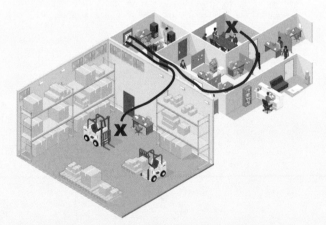

Review: Interpret Safety Warnings
12. Safety warning A means that employees in this area should watch out for forklifts driving and lifting material.

Answer Key

▶ **CHAPTER 1 (continued)**

13. Employees in this area would need to know which type of safety equipment to wear. If required to drive the forklift, employees would need to be trained on how to operate the steering mechanism and the lifting gears.
    - Students should circle the hard hat.
14. Safety warning B means that there is a danger of exposure to hazardous chemicals in that area.
15. Employees in this area should know what types of chemicals they may be exposed to and what safety equipment they should wear to protect themselves.
    - Students should circle the protective glasses.
16. Safety warning C means that there is a danger of radiation exposure in this area.
17. Employees in this area would need to wear protective equipment and radiation exposure badges to make sure they are not overexposed.
    - Students should circle the lead apron.

Review: Determine Wages, Deductions, and Take-Home Pay
18.

Name: _Student_

Week Ending: 6/13

Day	Morning		Afternoon		Total
	In	Out	In	Out	
Monday	8:55 AM	12:25 PM	12:55 PM	5:25 PM	8
Tuesday	8:45 AM	12:15 PM			3.5
Wednesday	8:45 AM	12:45 PM	1:40 PM	5:25 PM	7.75
Thursday			12:35 PM	5:35 PM	5
Friday	8:50 AM	12:05 PM	1:35 PM	5:50 PM	7.5
Saturday	9:05 AM	1:35 PM			4.5
				Total	36.25

Name: _Student_

Week Ending: 6/13

Earnings	Deductions
_36.25_ x $9.75 = _353.44_	Taxes.................$39.68
Hrs Worked Rate Gross Wages	401(k)..................$18.04
	Health Insurance......$21.64
	Total Deductions _79.36_

_353.44_	–	_79.36_	=	_274.08_
Gross Wages		Total Deductions		Net Wages

▶ **CHAPTER 2**

PAGES 36–37
ACTIVITY: *Professional Behaviors*
Students should circle the following behaviors: *communicating with a co-worker, folding clothes,* and *helping a customer at the cash register.*
Students should draw an X over the following behaviors: *socializing with a co-worker, texting during work hours, wearing clothes you would wear to a nightclub,* and *arriving late to work.*

PAGE 38
VIDEO 3: *Be On Guard*
1. Quanda and Joseph mentioned co-workers and patients by name and talked about their personal issues.
2. Quanda and Joseph gossiped about Naomi and Manuel, two co-workers who they believe are having an affair.
3. Answers will vary.

PAGE 39
ACTIVITY: *Personal or Professional*
1. Professional
2. Personal
3. Personal

PAGE 41
ACTIVITY: *The Group Dynamic*
1. Students should respond honestly about their performance during the group project. Students should identify their actions as being more like a leader or a follower.
2. Students should respond honestly about whether they performed the task to the best of their ability or whether they allowed others to do the work for them.
3. Students should respond honestly about whether they controlled the project or allowed others to participate to their fullest potential.
4. Students should respond honestly about how they felt when working with the group. They should also judge whether their group worked together successfully.

PAGE 43
ACTIVITY: *Going It Alone*
1. Students should respond honestly about their performance during the individual project.

Before You Begin

When you start a new job, you bring all of your previous experiences with you. These experiences may be from other jobs, school, volunteer work, or even your personal life. You may have a long list of positive behaviors that you can imitate to perform your new job well. You may also have some negative behaviors that you wish to learn from and leave behind.

Before you begin *Effective Employee,* reflect on the questions below and write your answers on the lines provided. These questions will help you find lasting success in your new job.

▶ **What steps will you take to prepare for your new job?**

_____

_____

_____

▶ **What aspects of the job are you most looking forward to?**

_____

_____

_____

Q *What did you do differently at this job than at your jobs in the past?*

A [In this job] I talk to clients—they have the same problems I had. They can't get or keep a job. Some of them have a criminal background, which makes it harder to find work. It makes me feel good to give back. If it wasn't for the program, I don't know where I would be. I was doing things my way, on the streets, and this slowed me down. I learned that I was important and that I did want to do something with my life.

Q *You have your high school diploma. Are you planning on furthering your education in the future?*

A Yes! Right now, I'm getting my certification in office management. After that, I'll keep working on my AA [Associate of Arts degree]. I want to be a paralegal. I don't know where I'd be without this program … I am always encouraging other people to come into the program. I speak to the classes and let them know what I went through. A lot of them are in the same situation I was in, and I let them know how it helped me and got me to where I am today.

Career Highlights

- Graduated from high school

- Attended Paxen Learning's work-readiness training, 2000

- Gained employment after attending training

- Secured her current Customer Service Representative job, 2009

- Taking classes at Northwest Florida State College

- Hopes to become a partner in a law firm

"I am at a real great place. I have this program to thank for that."

—Lashunda Thomas

Effective Employees in Action

Lashunda Thomas
Customer Service Representative
JobsPlus One-Stop

Effective employees are not born—they are made. Work-readiness training helps workers from all backgrounds learn to become good employees. Training programs and materials help new employees learn what to expect when starting a job. They also teach employees how to work effectively with supervisors and co-workers by emphasizing vital employability skills such as customer service and professionalism.

In 2000, Lashunda Thomas took the initiative to enroll in work-readiness training classes. Through this training, Lashunda became a very effective employee. Let's find out how she did it:

"I talk to clients—they have the same problems I had. They can't get or keep a job. It makes me feel good to give back."

Q *Good morning, Lashunda! If you could, please describe the work-readiness program you attended.*

A I came in as a high school graduate and a single mom with a new baby. It was tough. At first, I didn't want to do it. But I am so glad I did. It helped me be where I am today. It helped me overcome my situation. It taught me how to be a good employee.

Q *How did the skills you learned in the program help you improve your approach in the workplace?*

A I didn't know how to work with management before. The jobs I had in the past were dead ends because I didn't know how to manage my time. If I was late, I just wouldn't call or wouldn't go because I was scared. I learned how to overcome that and speak up for myself.

Q *What were you doing before you enrolled in the work-readiness program?*

A The jobs I had weren't working out. I didn't know how to be an effective employee. I thought it was just a job. I would show up, do what I wanted to do. If it didn't work out, I would just get another one. I learned that if you keep doing that, eventually no one will hire you. I never looked at it like that before.

Q *After you completed your work-readiness training, you landed a job at the career center. What happened during your first few days on the job?*

A [The first days] were crazy, but I got through it. I just kept reaching back to what I learned about how to be an effective employee—I can be counted on.

Chapter Review Activities

Chapter review activities allow students to participate in real-life workplace scenarios. These scenarios include completing an employee evaluation, writing a mentoring checklist, and taking and leaving phone messages.

1 These activities allow learners to prove mastery in several areas assessed by common workplace standards.

2 In addition to meeting standards, activities also offer students practical workplace experience.

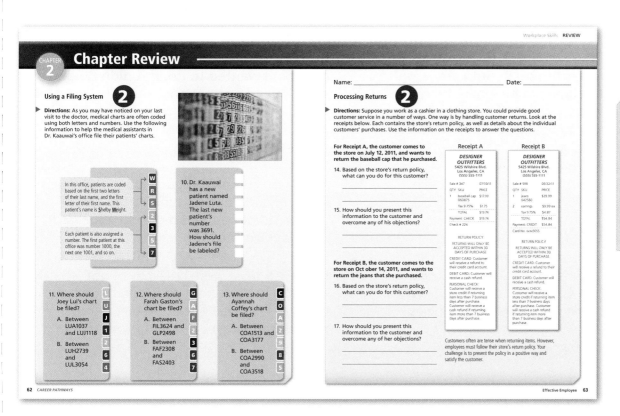

Chapter Recaps and Reviews

Each chapter concludes with a recap checklist designed to ensure learner mastery. The chapter review that follows allows students to assess their knowledge of workplace concepts. These pages can be removed and submitted for assessment purposes.

① The recap checklist highlights student goals for each lesson.

② The items on each lesson checklist mirror the goals set out for the learners at the beginning of that lesson.

③ The first page of the chapter review contains several types of questions: matching, short answer, true or false, and multiple choice.

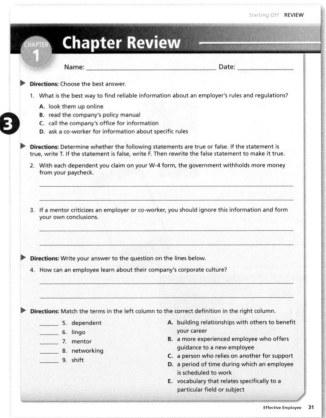

Pathways Features

Each chapter highlights one essential work-related topic in a special Pathways feature. These features offer in-depth information about how topics introduced in the chapter impact specific career areas.

1 Pathways features allow students to explore workplace concepts with their own career goals in mind.

2 Activities within these features offer students hands-on experience using workplace technology and skills.

For the Learner

Effective Employee equips emerging professionals with the skills, experiences, and intangibles to excel and advance in today's workplace. An engaging narrative and high-interest features will help you unlock the secrets to lasting success. *Effective Employee* contains several different components designed to enhance your learning experience.

❸ Multiple features highlight and provide further information about specific work-readiness skills. Feature titles include Communication, Technology, Leadership and Teamwork, Problem Solving/ Critical Thinking, Ethics and Legal Responsibilities.

❶ Each lesson begins with a list of student achievement goals and key employment terms.

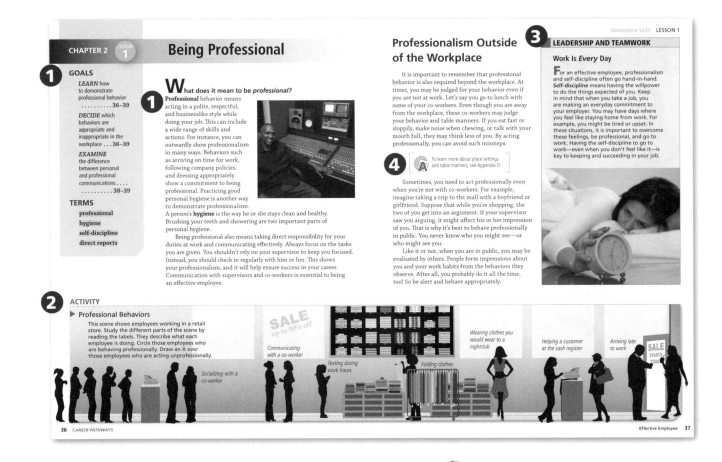

❷ Interactive activities offer students insights into appropriate workplace behaviors.

❹ The ⒶAPPENDIX indicates that learners can find more information about this topic in the appendices in the back of the book.

CAREER Pathways

The Next Generation of Work-Readiness Materials

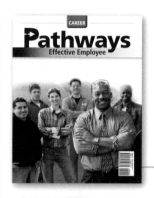

▶ *Effective Employee*

Effective Employee equips emerging professionals with the skills, experiences, and intangibles to excel and advance in today's workplace. An engaging narrative and high-interest features help learners unlock the secrets to lasting success.

▶ *Job Search*

Job Search removes the mystery—and guesswork—from the employment process. Learners receive instruction in key areas—from authoring résumés and cover letters to refining interviewing and negotiating skills—critical to employment success.

▶ *Document Literacy*

In *Document Literacy*, we put fine print under the microscope. A series of detailed callouts help learners decode and master complex consumer, personal, business, and financial documents. Chapter reviews allow learners to check understanding.

▶ *Financial Literacy*

For many, the world of personal finance sometimes can feel impersonal. Enter *Financial Literacy*, a color consumable title that helps learners personalize personal finance by emphasizing the essential areas of earning, spending, saving, and investing.

About Career Pathways

What do you want to be when you grow up? It's an innocent question, one often asked of schoolchildren. Increasingly, though, as our economy changes—and with it, entire industries—people of all ages are asking the same question. From children to young adults and on to older professionals and dislocated workers, more people than ever are attempting to find their way in today's workplace.

Often, the journey begins after high school. Whether they earn a diploma or a GED credential, potential employees often lack the proper support and guidance to make the transition from school to the workplace.

Adding to the challenge, workplaces themselves are changing. Traditional industries that once employed generations of workers have struggled to survive. Amid intense competition for available jobs, job seekers who lack necessary certifications or degrees and/or soft and career-specific skills struggle to find lasting success. Today's workers face a number of specific challenges. For example:

- Many workers, though highly skilled, may lack a market for their services.

- Although workers may have years of on-the-job experience, they could be unaware of current job-seeking techniques, such as using the Internet and in-person networking.

- Similarly, job seekers may lack a current, polished resume or sharp interviewing skills.

The solution to these challenges can be quite complex. To help people determine their next steps, Paxen offers its newest series, *Career Pathways*. This product line provides learners with strategies to survive—and thrive—in a 21st-century workforce.

Titles such as *Transitions, Job Search,* and *Greener Pastures: A Guide to Eco-Friendly Employment* aid learners in exploring and narrowing options. Others, such as *Effective Employee, Document Literacy,* and *Financial Literacy*, provide strategies for excelling inside and outside of the workplace.

Career Pathways was built in accordance with the work-readiness competencies listed in the table below.

COMPETENCIES

Pathways Essential Knowledge and Skill Statements	National Standards in K-12 Personal Finance Education
CASAS	Workforce Investment Act (WIA) Elements
Equipped for the Future (EFF)	21st Century Skills
National Career Development Guidelines (NCDG)	Pre-Employment and Work Maturity (PEWM)

67
Employers appreciate and value effective employees. They show this by thanking them, providing salary increases, and giving awards.

94
Effective employees work well in groups and on their own.

Table of Contents

8
Employers provide information about workplace policies, procedures, and training.

20
New employees often are paired with mentors for on-the-job training.

37 (alarm clock) iStockphoto © Duard van der Westhuizen; 38 (computer mouse) iStockphoto © Luis Carlos Torres; (women using laptop) iStockphoto © quavondo 39 (woman on computer) iStockphoto © absolut_100; (doctor and nurse) Getty Images © Thinkstock Images; (couple having an intense discussion) iStockphoto © Brett Mulcahy 40 (diverse group) iStockphoto © Chris Schmidt 41 (group doing puzzle) © Paxen Learning – special thanks to Amy Smallwood, Veronica Massa, Shannon McGregor, and Taylor Vaughan; (puzzle illustration) iStockphoto 42 (pizza chef) iStockphoto © Imageegaml 43 (origami) © Paxen Learning – special thanks to Nicholas Harrison; (records administrator) iStockphoto © DenGuy 44 (teamwork—shaking hands) iStockphoto © Jacob Wackerhausen; (welcoming boss) iStockphoto © Jacob Wackerhausen; (smiling female boss) iStockphoto © claudiobaba; (African American business man) iStockphoto © Nicholas Monu 45 (group working together) iStockphoto © DaveBolton; (woman in group) iStockphoto © Jacob Wackerhausen 46 (silhouettes) iStockphoto 47 (women in office) Getty Images © Sean Justice; (men arguing) iStockphoto © Cliff Parnell; (colleagues reviewing MRI) Getty Images © Jose Luis Pelaez Inc. 48 (surgeons in corridor) Getty Images © Dana Neely 49 (multigenerational medical personnel) Getty Images © Ken Fisher 50 (hair stylist) iStockphoto © niknikon; (construction worker and architect) Getty Images © Andersen Ross 51 (MRI machine) Getty Images © Alvis Upitis; (woman selecting seafood) Getty Images © Michael Blann; (IT silhouettes) iStockphoto 52 (customer on cell phone) iStockphoto © GMosher; (restaurant manager on cell phone) iStockphoto © Simon Krzic 53 (restaurant check) iStockphoto © DNY59; (man paying restaurant bill) Getty Images © Jochen Sand 54 (pill bottle) © Paxen Learning; (nurse and patient) Getty Images © Jose Luis Pelaez; (wheelbarrow) Getty Images © Brand X Pictures; (plants and shrubs) Getty Images © Dave King; (man with clipboard) iStockphoto © wdstock 55 (calculator) © Paxen Learning; (supermarket checkout) Getty Images © Ariel Skelley; (woman working on computer) © Paxen Learning – special thanks to Danielle Gilbert 56 (car accident) Getty Images © Chris Ryan 57 (silhouettes) iStockphoto; (man jogging) iStockphoto © Ryan Lane; (woman at park) iStockphoto © Sheriar Irani; (man listening to music) Shutterstock © Monkey Business Images; (woman at church) iStockphoto © Andres Balcazar; (women talking) iStockphoto © Miroslav Ferkuniak 58 (airline ticket counter) Getty Images © Glow Images; (flight attendant) Getty Images © Jonnie Miles 59 (male kitchen workers) Getty Images © Smith Collection; (chef and servers) Getty Images © Dex Image; (woman working in woodshop) Getty Images © Hill Street Studios; (women talking in workshop) Getty Images © ColorBlind Images 62 (filing system) iStockphoto © Teresa Pigeon 64 (telephone) iStockphoto © Khuong Hoang; (memo pad) © Paxen Learning 65 (silhouettes) iStockphoto 66 (father and son) iStockphoto © Adam Kazmierski; (young couple) iStockphoto © Catherine Yeulet; (woman graduating) iStockphoto © Jason Stitt 67 (employee of the month) Getty Images © Fuse; (wind turbine) Getty Images © Jupiterimages 68 (vials of blood) iStockphoto © Robert Byron; (phlebotomist) Getty Images © Tetra Images; (blood extraction) iStockphoto © Picsfive; (blood bag) iStockphoto © Timothey Kosachev; (lollipop) iStockphoto © James Trice; (bottle of orange juice) iStockphoto © Susan Trigg; (glass of orange juice) iStockphoto © Joanna Pecha; (syringe) iStockphoto © Sven Hoppe 69 (tow truck driver) Getty Images © Bill Losh; (hotel maid) Getty Images © Thinkstock Images 70 (dental lab) iStockphoto © Robert Kneschke; (counseling session) iStockphoto © Lisa F. Young 71 (silhouettes) iStockphoto; (upset employees) Getty Images © Jetta Productions 72 (silhouettes) iStockphoto; (restaurant manager and chef) Getty Images © Andersen Ross 73 (upset customer) iStockphoto © Stockphoto4u; (owner of firm) iStockphoto © Don Bayley; (contractor) iStockphoto © Denis Pepin; (tile layer) iStockphoto © usas; (mechanics) Getty Images © Joselito Briones 74 (gossiping employees) iStockphoto © Jen Grantham 75 (retail workers hanging shirts) iStockphoto © vm 76 (performance review) iStockphoto © Josh Rinehults 77 (female employee) iStockphoto © Keith Binns; (male employee) iStockphoto © Jane Norton 78 (silhouettes) iStockphoto 79 (map) Mapping Specialists; (silhouettes) iStockphoto 83 (business meeting) iStockphoto © nyul 84 (silhouettes) iStockphoto 85 (silhouettes) iStockphoto 87 (factory workers) Getty Images © Jetta Productions 88 (group of employees) © Paxen Learning – special thanks to Kelly Hackett, Chris Stone, Michael Walker, and Marty Giblin 89 (silhouettes) iStockphoto 90 (male and female employee) © Paxen Learning – special thanks to Jennifer Torres and Michael Walker 91 (silhouettes) iStockphoto 93 (circuit board) iStockphoto © Eduard Andras; (handshake) iStockphoto © Dennis Owusu-Ansah; (diploma) © Paxen Learning; (happy family) iStockphoto © Rosemarie Gearhart 94 (silhouettes) iStockphoto; (medical personnel) Getty Images © Gary John Norman; (office scene) iStockphoto © Chris Schmidt; (woman receiving certificate) Getty Images © Image Source 95 (silhouettes) iStockphoto 97 (baker frosting cake) Getty Images © Alexa Miller; (dental assistant) Getty Images © Karin Dreyer; (policeman) Getty Images © Thinkstock 98 (graphic designers working on computer) iStockphoto © mümin inan 99 (woman in library) iStockphoto © René Mansi 100 (dreaming student) Shutterstock © aldegonde; (student in ten years) iStockphoto © Nicholas Monu; (collecting evidence) iStockphoto © 36clicks; (ballistic analysis) iStockphoto © biffspandex; (crime scene) iStockphoto © 36clicks; (fingerprints) iStockphoto © Hans Laubel 101 (evidence shell casing) iStockphoto © James Ferrie; (various CSI in table) iStockphoto © Brandon Alms 102 (witness testifying) iStockphoto © Alina Solovyova-Vincent 104 (silhouettes) iStockphoto 105 (illustration) iStockphoto; (boss and introverted employee) © Paxen Learning – special thanks to Steve Jacoby and Adelina Crivello; (boss and extroverted employee) © Paxen Learning – special thanks to Steve Jacoby and Shannon McGregor 106 (employee meeting) © Paxen Learning – special thanks to Taylor Vaughan, Adelina Crivello, and Shannon McGregor 107 (Employee meeting) © Paxen Learning – special thanks to Jenifer Harrison, Chris Taylor, Katherine Martin, Lloyd Carthon; (Employee meeting – new leader) © Paxen Learning – special thanks to Jenifer Harrison, Chris Taylor, Larry Pike, Lloyd Carthon 108 (mentor) Getty Images © GLG3 109 (doctors mentoring) iStockphoto © Константин Чагин; (mentor active listening) iStockphoto © Pali Rao 110 (Farm workers conferring) iStockphoto © David Jones 111 (manager) iStockphoto © Laser222; (silhouettes) iStockphoto 112 (management challenges) © Paxen Learning – special thanks to Kolbie Rittenhouse and Chris Taylor; (store clerk using laptop) Getty Images © Marc Romanelli 113 (preschool classroom) iStockphoto © Hongqi Zhang 116 (young mother with infant) Adobe Stock Photo 118 (manager serving customer) Getty Images © Image Source; (oil change worker) iStockphoto © Diego Cuervo 119 (two co-workers arguing) iStockphoto © Brad Killer 123 (formal place setting) iStockphoto © philipp_g 124 (silhouette) iStockphoto

Acknowledgements

▶ **Acknowledgements**

Dave Potter
Lashunda Thomas
Mary Lou Reed, Executive Director, Workforce Development Board of Okaloosa and Walton Counties
Linda Sumblin, COO, Workforce Development Board of Okaloosa and Walton Counties
Amy Aldridge, Vice-President, Eaton National Bank and Trust

CAREER

Pathways

Effective Employee

STARTING OFF | WORKPLACE SKILLS | JOB PERFORMANCE | SUCCESS ON THE JOB

PAXEN
Learning Corporation

Melbourne, Florida
www.paxen.com